# THE 8 HABITS
## OF A HIGHLY EFFECTIVE SAFETY CULTURE

# THE 8 HABITS
## OF A HIGHLY EFFECTIVE SAFETY CULTURE

Powerful Lessons in Human Performance

**ROD COURTNEY**

*gatekeeper press*
Columbus, Ohio

The views and opinions expressed in this book are solely those of the author and do not necessarily reflect the views or opinions of Gatekeeper Press. Gatekeeper Press is not to be held responsible for and expressly disclaims responsibility of the content herein.

THE 8 HABITS OF A HIGHLY EFFECTIVE SAFETY CULTURE
*Powerful Lessons in Human Performance*

Published by Gatekeeper Press
2167 Stringtown Rd, Suite 109
Columbus, OH 43123-2989
www.GatekeeperPress.com

Copyright © 2022 by Rod Courtney

All rights reserved. Neither this book, nor any parts within it may be sold or reproduced in any form or by any electronic or mechanical means, including information storage and retrieval systems, without permission in writing from the author. The only exception is by a reviewer, who may quote short excerpts in a review.

The cover design, interior formatting, typesetting, and editorial work for this book are entirely the product of the author. Gatekeeper Press did not participate in and is not responsible for any aspect of these elements.

Library of Congress Control Number: 2022933994

ISBN (paperback): 9781662926181
eISBN: 9781662926198

# CONTENTS

| | |
|---|---|
| FOREWORD | 3 |
| ACKNOWLEDGEMENTS | 5 |
| INTRODUCTION: HOW IT ALL STARTED | 9 |
| **HABIT #1**: STOP MAKING SAFETY A PRIORITY | 27 |
| **HABIT #2**: MAKE IT SAFE FOR PEOPLE TO RAISE CONCERNS | 33 |
| **HABIT #3**: MAKE SAFETY THE RESPONSIBILITY OF OPERATIONS | 43 |
| **HABIT #4**: FOCUS LEFT OF ZERO | 55 |
| **HABIT #5**: STOP MANAGING PEOPLE | 63 |
| **HABIT #6**: STOP TRYING TO FIX THE WORKER | 71 |
| **HABIT #7**: FIND THE STCKY & STOP THE SIF | 99 |
| **HABIT #8**: TRYING TO INFLUENCE EVERYONE | 107 |
| THE INCOMPLETE LIST | 125 |
| AUTHOR BIO | 129 |
| REFERENCES | 130 |

## FOREWORD

It's been an honor to partner with Rod as a colleague over the past several years and most importantly, to call him a friend.

---

Always a gentleman and a scholar, Rod has a passion for ensuring the well-being of everyone he meets. When first meeting on a project several years ago, as fellow military veterans we quickly realized the common interests we shared; it was evident then that Rod is wise beyond his years in his ability to speak to others at their levels of understanding to ensure meaningful conversations in any regard. It didn't take long to recognize his depth of thought, wisdom rooted in his passion, and uncanny ability to draw on personal experiences to make even the most obscure Health and Safety concepts relatable.

As an emerging thought leader in Health and Safety, Rod's accomplishments include hands-on safety leadership, subject matter expertise, and selfless sharing of information in public speaking engagements in his efforts for all to attain premier Occupational Safety knowledge in their respective fields.

As an extension thereof, in this book, Rod cleverly overlays an arsenal of life experiences atop proven means and methods to help prevent injuries in the workplace and contribute to safe execution of construction activities in any capacity. Although many of these principles have stand-alone value, added to any health and safety program, Rod, by way of his personal experiences, overlays a one-of-a-kind perspective, to ensure safety insofar as possible, just as when he is a safety leader on a project and in his public speaking engagements.

What Rod brings to any table speaks volumes in what he has pulled together in *8 Habits* and offers even greater value for whomever has the pleasure of reading this book. More specifically, Rod helps demystify timeless deep domain safety principles that will contribute to the success of any safety program. His conversational and approachable style is well-suited for any board room or turbine deck alike. In either regard or for all in between, Rod's integrity above all else shows through from page 1 just as when having the opportunity of meeting him in person.

By way of the sharing of his journey through career experiences over the years, he offers real-life examples for all readers to be able to build upon when sharing the same principles with their teams. Whether the well-seasoned safety leader or those new to the industry, it's with high confidence that I feel there will be something of value for all safety leaders to leverage as he breaks down leading health and safety principles in a most clever way. A proponent of iron sharpening iron, the wealth of knowledge Rod has pulled together in *8 Habits* has been a great tool to sharpen the knives for me and I hope the same for you as you read this soon-to-be HSE timeless classic.

Rod, congratulations on the wonderful accomplishment in this book; my knives are sharper for it, challenge accepted, and I'm honored on all fronts to be part of this journey with you.

**Jason Castro**, CSP, CUSP

## ACKNOWLEDGEMENTS

The information in this book has taken nearly two decades to put together and so many people have contributed to my ability and knowledge to be able to write it and share these principles with you.

First, this book is dedicated to Tommy R. Graham. Mr. Tommy was the first person to give me a chance in a safety role. He was my first mentor and truly took me under his wing as a young safety professional and guided me through the nuances of making safety important in a time when safety was viewed as a hit on the bottom line with no return on investment. Mr. Tommy passed away August 24, 2018, and while he left a hole in the lives of his family and friends that can never be filled, the number of lives he touched over the years is something that can't be measured.

I would like to thank the KBR LogCAP III leadership and training team for starting me on the path of writing these powerful lessons in human performance. Without your sharing of knowledge, there is no way this book would have ever been written.

I want to thank my wife Christi for being supportive throughout the writing process and keeping our family and home together during all the years I spent traveling around the world gaining the knowledge and experience to put on these pages for you to learn and develop your own systems and safety culture.

A very special thank you to Todd Conklin, PhD. Dr. Conklin has been a blazing pioneer in the field of Human Performance and has helped transform so many companies from a "Safety First" mentality to a "Safety Differently" mentality. His research and personal experience have been absolutely critical to the development of not only this book, but also of countless safety cultures around the world.

Thank you to Jason Castro for always being a sounding board and colleague, and for taking the time to write the foreword to this book. You have always helped to keep me levelheaded and are someone I know I can trust to tell me the truth.

I want to thank David McPeak for writing his book *Frontline Leadership – The Hurdle*. The book has a wealth of knowledge and information for anyone in a leadership position or anyone wanting to better develop their leadership skills. But David is the one who convinced me to finish this book after all these years and for that I am truly grateful.

Shortly before starting to write this book for the final time, I joined TikTok, and one of the very first people that inspired me was First Sergeant Deantoni Littleton, A.K.A. Dirtybirdfitness. He uses a phrase that I have used over my career both in and out of the military: "Humanize the rank." Those three words hold so much meaning. I wish more leaders would learn to do it. For a while, First Sargent Littleton was "The Official First Sergeant of TikTok." Since then, he has been assigned as an ROTC instructor at the University of Ohio and now holds the rank of Master Sergeant. I know that's not a demotion, but you'll always be "Top" to me. Thanks for being someone I try to emulate every day.

I want to also thank Jean Paul Courville, SGM, USMC (RET). Jean Paul and I grew up in the same small town and were friends in high school. We graduated from the same school and both chose the military as our path afterwards. I served eight years in the Army and JP served 20+ in the Marine

Corps. He grew into one of the best leaders I have ever known and has inspired me so many times throughout my life. Thank you for your selfless service to our great country; but more than that, thank you for always being the example.

Over the years, there have been so many people who have taught me and influenced the professional I am today. Because I don't want to list names and possibly leave someone out, this final acknowledgement goes to everyone who has helped me learn when I needed to learn, allowed me to fail when I needed to fail, and cleared the path for me to be successful.

## INTRODUCTION
# HOW IT ALL STARTED

I began writing this book in 2004 while working as a civilian contractor for Kellogg Brown & Root (KBR) in Iraq.

I was the Area HSE Manager for a large portion of the Logistical Civilian Augmentation Program #3 (LogCAP III) Project. Our contract required us to hire a certain percentage of local national employees (Iraqis) to help build bases for the US military and coalition forces. This was to help the local economies and to teach the Iraqi people new skills that they could use once we were gone. In theory, this was a great idea; however, in reality, it was a safety nightmare. Being a U.S. based company, we were required to follow O.S.H.A. 29 CFR 1926 (Construction), O.S.H.A. 29 CFR 1910 (General Industry), and in some cases U.S. Army Corp of Engineers EM 385. But none of this translated to the "Idha Sh Allah" way of life in this part of the world. Idha Sh Allah is loosely translated to "God Willing" in English and is pronounced "en shallah." Without turning this into a discussion of religion, I just need you to understand that many in this part of the world believe they have no control over the things that happen to them. So, bring this culture to an American construction site and I'm sure you can see the difficulties.

The first day, we started to build a new dining facility and a brand-new crew of locals from the city of Balad came to work. Only a small number wore shoes and most of those were sandals. So like any good company would, we issued them coveralls, safety-toed boots, safety glasses, hard hats, gloves and, in some cases, N95 dust masks. They were like kids on Christmas morning. I still don't believe I have ever seen a group of grown men so appreciative for anything in my life.

Then there was the language barrier. We had translators to help us, but some things just don't translate exactly from one language to another. For example: Once I was given the task of ordering fire extinguishers for every building on the base. If I remember correctly, it was 200+ 10 and 20 lb. fire extinguishers. I ordered them from a local businessman, who over the years ended up selling us tens of thousands of dollars' worth of goods. I didn't speak Arabic and he didn't speak English. So, we played charades and I acted out a fire and then putting it out with what was *obviously* a 20 lb. fire extinguisher. And, Nabil (the businessman) nodded and said "no problem" in perfect South Louisiana English. So, of course, I thought he understood and he left with an order for the extinguishers. A few days later, Nabil returned, driving a Nissan pick-up truck with a bed full of smoke detectors. Wait, what? As it turns out, neither of us were very good at charades and this language barrier issue would continue to be a problem for the entire three years I was there.

The second day of building the new dining facility, the highly motivated, much appreciative crew didn't show up on time. But eventually they came and NONE of them had any of the equipment we had issued to them the day before. They sold it! Every single piece! Even the cheap plastic safety glasses. And, without missing a beat, the translator told us, they know we have more in the "big red box" (this was a metal 20-foot Conex shipping container). So, this time, we issued them only what they needed and had them return it at the end of the day.

When my safety team would do their daily work observations and weekly inspections, we would have an insanely high number of unsafe behaviors, near misses, and safety violations, and the accident rates reflected the safety culture, or lack thereof. If it hadn't been for the obscene number of man-hours we logged each week, the project incident rates would have been triple that of any other US company.

So, like any good safety professional, I made it my life's mission to change a culture that had never even heard of workplace safety, much less had worked for an employer that insisted on it.

In extreme situations like this, you have to go back to the bare basics. I began to study safety cultures around the world from as far back as 1760 all the way through to current day cultures. And, come to find out, we were not that much different from the Iraqis in 2003-2006.

# HISTORY OF SAFETY CULTURE: U.S., EUROPE AND BRITAIN

## The Industrial Revolution 1760-1800s

(Revised from original, written by Don Cameron, StaySafe and used with his permission.[1])

Before the Industrial Revolution began in 1760, it was the norm to make a living through agriculture or by the making and selling of products from home. With new developments in machinery and manufacturing processes, the US, Europe and Britain began moving towards a society fueled by mass production and the factory system. People flocked to the cities for work where there were increased opportunities for employment in the new mills and factories. The vast number of people looking for work, and the need for cheap labor, led to poor pay, hazardous factory conditions and an increase in child labor. Hours were long and conditions dangerous, with many losing their lives at work. Work was particularly dangerous for children who would work from as young as four and sometimes over 12 hours a day. (Yes, you heard that correctly, four-year-old children working 12+ hours a day.) Many were instructed to climb under machinery which would often result in loss of limbs, while others were crushed and some decapitated. Girls working at match factories would develop phossy jaw from phosphorus fumes, children employed at glassworks were regularly burnt and blinded, while those working at potteries were vulnerable to poisonous clay dust. A lack of health and safety also meant that many children developed occupational diseases such as lung cancer.

*Picture from safetylineloneworker.com[2]*

## The Factory Act of 1802 (U.K.)

An outcry over child labor conditions led to factory owner, Sir Robert Peel, introducing the Health and Morals of Apprentices Act 1802, commonly known as the Factory Act. The Factory Act applied to all textile mills and factories employing three or more apprentices or twenty employees and required factories to:

- Have sufficient windows and opening for ventilation
- Be cleaned at least twice yearly with quicklime and water
- Limit working hours for apprentices to no more than 12 hours a day (excluding time taken for breaks)
- Stop night-time working by apprentices during the hours of 9 p.m. and 6 a.m.
- Provide suitable clothing and sleeping accommodation to every apprentice
- Instruct apprentices in reading, writing, arithmetic and the principles of the Christian religion

While limited to a small portion of the workforce and with limited enforcement, the Factory Act is generally seen as the beginning of health and safety regulation.[3]

*The Evolution of Safety - History of Workplace Safety (safetylineloneworker.com)*

# The Introduction of Factory Inspectors 1833-1868

Workers tired of spending over 12 hours a day in the factories began a movement to reduce working days to 10 hours, known as the "Ten Hours Movement." Pressure from the group led to the Factory Act of 1833. The Act extended the 12 hours working limit to all children and included wool and linen mills. Perhaps the most important development, however, was the introduction of factory inspectors. The inspectors were given access to the mills and granted permission to question workers. Their main duty was to prevent injury and overworking of child workers, but they were also able to formulate new regulations and laws to ensure the Factories Act could be suitably enforced. Despite only four inspectors being appointed for approximately 3,000 textile mills across the country, they were able to influence subsequent legislation relating to machinery guarding and accident reporting. A growing public interest in worker's welfare, influenced in part by popular writers such as Charles Dickens, saw inspector numbers grow to 35 in 1886. The type of workplaces they were able to enter also grew to cover the majority of workplaces.[4]

*The Evolution of Safety - History of Workplace Safety (safetylineloneworker.com)*

Today, OSHA is a small agency and they have approximately 1,850 inspectors, between federal and state agencies, and are "responsible for the health and safety of 130 million workers, employed at more than 8 million worksites around the nation — which translates to about one compliance officer for every 70,000 workers."[5]

So, if they worked seven days a week for 12 years, they could perform one inspection per worksite.

## The Introduction of "Duty of Care" in 1837

On May 30, 1835, Charles Priestley suffered a broken femur bone, dislocated shoulder and several other injuries after a wagon cracked and overturned due to overloading by his employer, Thomas Fowler, in the U.K. Priestly spent nineteen weeks recovering at a nearby inn, which cost him about $250 (US). Priestly sued Fowler for compensation relating to the accident — the first documented case of an employee suing an employer over work-related injuries. The jury awarded Priestley $500 in a landmark case which established the idea that employers owed their employees a duty of care. However, an appeal of the case established that the employer is not responsible to ensure higher safety standards for an employee than he ensures for himself.[6]

Photo Credit: Library of Congress, LC-DIG-nclc-01823

Written by Rod Courtney

*Photo Credit: Library of Congress, LC-DIG-nclc-01823*

## Safety Regulations Increase 1842-1878

Several acts introduced over the next 36 years, saw protection towards women and children strengthen. Women and children were prevented from working in underground mines, the use of child labor to clean and maintain moving machinery was stopped, and a 56-hour work week for women and children was introduced.[7]

*The Evolution of Safety - History of Workplace Safety (safetylineloneworker.com)*

## The Employer's Liability Act of 1880

In an attempt to correct the doctrine of Common Employment established following Priestley v. Fowler, the Employer's Liability Act enabled workers to seek compensation for injuries resulting from negligence of a fellow employee. The act states that any worker, or his family, are entitled to compensation for injury or death caused by a defect in equipment or machinery or negligence of a person given authority over the worker by the employer. The Workmen's Compensation Act of 1987 later removed the requirement that the injured party prove who was at fault for the injury and are instead required only to prove that the injury occurred on the job.[8]

## A Continued Increase in Acts and Reforms 1880-1970

Health and safety continued to flourish, with a number of acts and reforms improving upon health and safety regulation across the country. Employers were required to provide safeguarding for machinery, the legal working age was gradually raised and more and more inspectors were appointed across industries. 1878 even saw the first safeguarding put in place for those working in the agriculture industry, in regard to equipment, machinery and poisonous substances.[9]

*The Evolution of Safety - History of Workplace Safety (safetylineloneworker.com)*

Written by Rod Courtney

## And Then it Happened!

On December 29, 1970, President Richard M. Nixon signed The Occupational Safety and Health Act of 1970, also known as the Williams-Steiger Act in honor of the two men who pressed so hard for its passage.[10] Then, on April 28, 1971, the Occupational Health and Safety Administration was created *(29 U.S.C. §651 et seq. 1970)*.

*Executive Orders | Richard Nixon Museum and Library (nixonlibrary.gov)*[11]

Before we go any further with the evolution of safety cultures, I want you to imagine something. As I write this, it is February 2022. The current presidential administration signed an executive order to make Covid-19 vaccines mandatory for all companies with 100 or more employees. The Supreme Court just blocked the administration from enforcing its sweeping vaccine-or-test requirements for large private companies. The original order instructed OSHA to enforce the rule.

Many will read this and understand the turmoil this executive order created. Please understand, I am not discussing my personal political beliefs; I am only stating the facts.

Over the past six months, I have heard every theory you can imagine about why an administration would do this and if it is even legal. Political stances aside, how did it make you feel?

Now, let's go back to the 1960s and pretend you are a business owner. The company has been passed down for generations in your family and now you are the company head. In 1970, you hear mention of a possible executive order that will make it *your* responsibility to protect employees from hazards. This law will be enforced by a new government agency called the Occupational Safety and Health Administration (OSHA). That's right; the federal government is going to fine your company if you don't follow these new rules.

*How can they do that? The government is overreaching its authority! This is just another way for politicians to make money! They can't tell me what to do; this is a free country!*

I think you get my point. Can you imagine the turmoil this executive order created? Now imagine if it had failed. Personally, I am not a big supporter of "More Government," but in my opinion, this order was absolutely needed. Now let's get back to our evolution of safety culture history lesson.

**1970s**
In the beginning, company philosophies were simple: "Don't get hurt."

The first citation written by OSHA was to Gimbel Brothers Department Store in New York City. They found two violations and, while a citation was written, no fine was issued.

## Inspection Detail

**Inspection: 11593639 - Gimbel Brothers Inc**

**Inspection Information - Office: Inactive-New York**

| | | |
|---|---|---|
| Nr: 11593639 | Report ID: 0235200 | Open Date: 08/04/1972 |
| Gimbel Brothers Inc | | |
| 1275 Broadway | | Union Status: NonUnion |
| New York City, NY 10001 | | |
| SIC: 5311/Department Stores | | |
| Inspection Type: | Complaint | |
| Scope: | Partial | Advanced Notice: |
| Ownership: | | |
| Safety/Health: | Safety | Close Conference: 08/04/1972 |
| | | Close Case: 03/10/1984 |

### Violation Summary

| | Serious | Willful | Repeat | Other | Unclass | Total |
|---|---|---|---|---|---|---|
| Initial Violations | | | | 2 | | 2 |
| Current Violations | | | | 2 | | 2 |
| Initial Penalty | $0 | $0 | $0 | $0 | $0 | $0 |
| Current Penalty | $0 | $0 | $0 | $0 | $0 | $0 |
| FTA Amount | $0 | $0 | $0 | $0 | $0 | $0 |

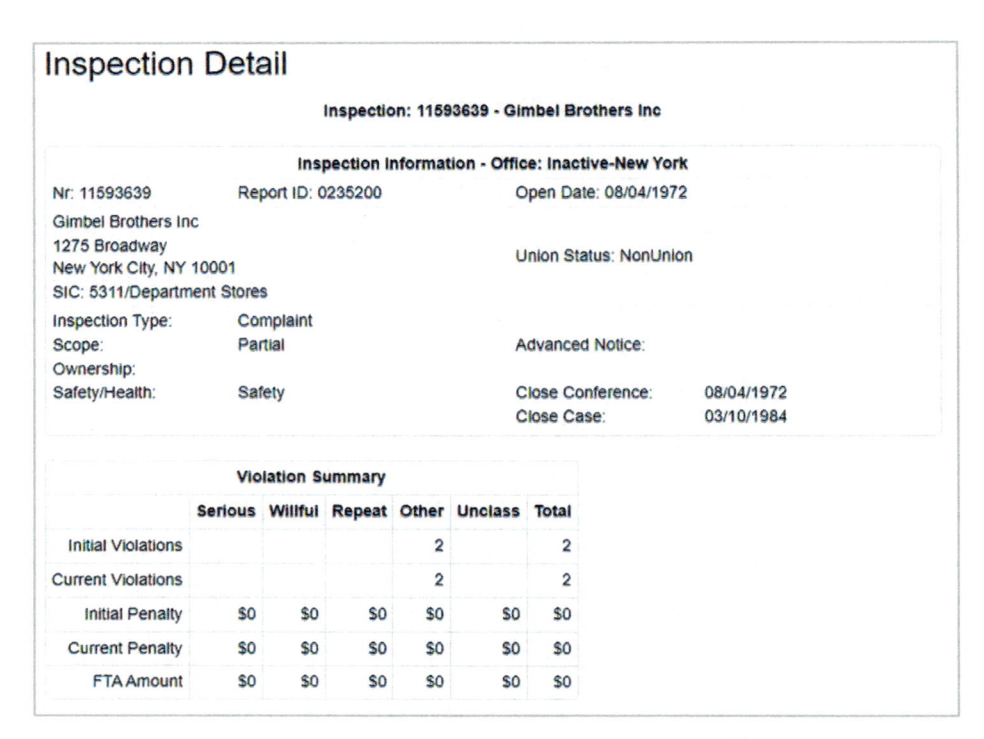

*FIG – 0 Record of Inspection August 4, 1972*[12]

The first fine was issued on October 23, 1972, to Diane, Inc., a manufacturing company in Manhattan, for $45 (equivalent of about $300 today). It was then that the new philosophy became "Get caught getting hurt and get fired." While this did have a profound effect on the way companies viewed employee safety and helped reduce the number of accidents, we found out later that it was counterproductive.

| Inspection Information - Office: Manhattan |||||||
|---|---|---|---|---|---|---|
| Nr: 11777042 | Report ID: 0215000 | | | Open Date: 10/23/1972 |||
| Diane Inc | | | | |||
| 165 West 25th Street | | | | Union Status: NonUnion |||
| New York City, NY 10001 | | | | |||
| SIC: 2290 | | | | |||
| Inspection Type: | Planned | | | |||
| Scope: | Complete | | | Advanced Notice: |||
| Ownership: | | | | |||
| Safety/Health: | Safety | | | Close Conference: | 10/23/1972 ||
| Planning Guide: | Safety-Manufacturing | | | Close Case: | 03/10/1984 ||

| Violation Summary ||||||
|---|---|---|---|---|---|
| | Serious | Willful | Repeat | Other | Unclass | Total |
|---|---|---|---|---|---|---|
| Initial Violations | | | | 1 | | 1 |
| Current Violations | | | | 1 | | 1 |
| Initial Penalty | $0 | $0 | $0 | $45 | $0 | $45 |
| Current Penalty | $0 | $0 | $0 | $45 | $0 | $45 |
| FTA Amount | $0 | $0 | $0 | $0 | $0 | $0 |

*FIG – 00 Record of inspection October 23, 1972*[13]

## 1980s

Somewhere around 1980, the new company philosophy became "Accident occurs, discipline employee, create new policy and enforce the new policy." Then when another accident happens, it starts all over again.

Accident – Discipline – Create New Policy – Enforce New Policy

## 1990s

So, in the early 1990s, we started doing more "Behavior-Based Safety" (BBS). While the Ford Motor Company was the first company on record to use the BBS model, DuPont developed the first widely utilized BBS program called Dupont S.T.O.P. (Safety Training Observation Program). Now, for over 30 years, we've been trying to fix the workers' behaviors in order to avoid an accident.

Written by Rod Courtney

# BEHAVIOR-BASED SAFETY ORIGIN

During the 1930s, an insurance investigator named H.W. Heinrich did a study of the causes of workplace accidents. His conclusion was that 88% of all workplace accidents and injuries were caused by "unsafe acts." He arrived at this conclusion by studying thousands of accident reports.[14]

The Heinrich Triangle became the basis for what is now known as Behavior Based Safety. The idea is to focus on the bottom of the triangle (Unsafe Acts and Conditions) and you will avoid the top of the triangle (Minor Incidents) all the way to a "Fatality."

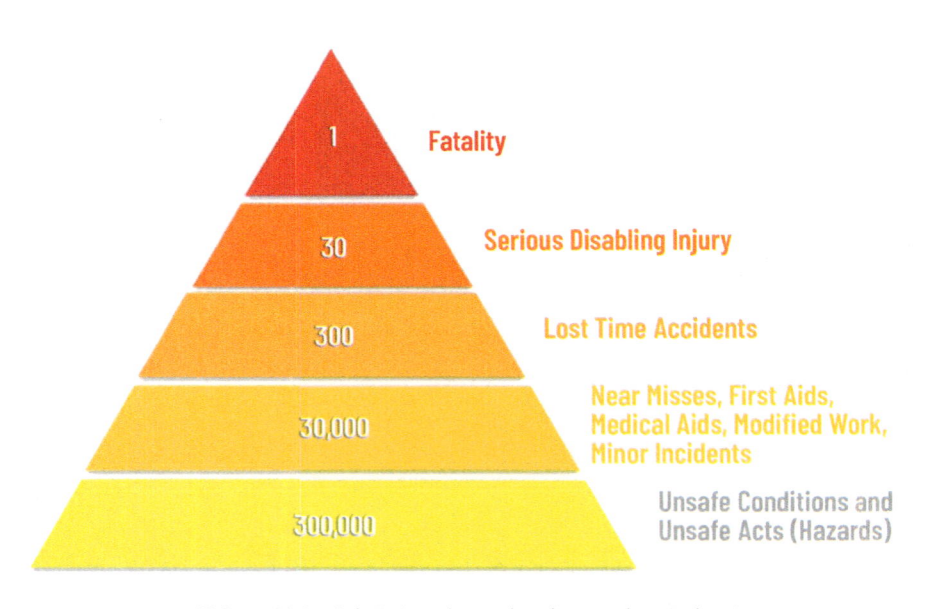

*FIG 1 - Heinrich Triangle – The theory that Behavior Based Safety was built from*

And, while there is some truth to this, the information Mr. Heinrich collected has come under scrutiny and, overall, it is not a sustainable method for reducing accidents. (Before you BBS fanatics throw this book in the trash, I will explain this in great detail in chapter six.)

The 8 Habits of a Highly Effective Safety Culture

While every previous safety culture had its place in time and ultimately did help us get to where we are, the **only** way we will ever progress is through continuous improvement. Today, as we have learned from the past and truly begun to study human nature, we start to understand why people do what they do. So now we use a Human Performance approach. The Human Performance approach uses safety observations and expands on them, then changes the way we look at human behavior and errors altogether. More on this later, but for now, let's go back to Iraq in 2004.

## MIDDLE OF SUMMER, TIKRIT, IRAQ

So, there we were, building a small city and all of its connected infrastructure, using craft labor that had never been required to do anything safely, much less follow regulations like 29 CFR. If there is one thing I have learned over the years, it is that people do not like change. Mark Twain said it best: *"The only person who likes change is a wet baby,"* and he could not be more correct. So, in order to create a sustainable safety culture without alienating those who would resist change, we had to start small and move slowly. Which, as many of you know, is not how a U.S. safety professional tends to act. We see something wrong and it gets fixed. We see two or three or even four things wrong and they all get fixed before the end of the day. That wouldn't work in our environment in Iraq, so we started small, with safety-toed boots.

We had our translators explain the reason why we wear them and showed pictures of people who didn't wear them and, although we still required them to "leave them at the gate" at the end of the day, they understood we were doing this because we cared about them and their families. Once that trust was built, the next steps were easier. When I left Iraq in 2006, after three years of doing construction work in an active combat zone with craft labor that, in the beginning, didn't care about their own personal safety much less that of their coworkers, I noticed some trends. Things that worked and things that didn't. This is when I realized that there are specific things (habits) that will systematically change a culture into one of sustainable, injury-free forward progression.

In full disclosure, I first wrote all eight of these down in 2006 and, as I write this book in 2021, five of the original eight habits are the same. To this day, they are the foundation on which I have developed numerous programs and management systems. I am not so egotistical to believe that none of these habits will ever change again. So I want everyone to be open to new ideas and to change. Let this book be a tool, a guide if you will. Write in it. Highlight things that you think are important. Scratch through things that change in the years to come and replace them with what works best for you and your organization. Then read it again and see what's changed. Always strive for continuous improvement and keep your greatest asset (your employees) safe.

## WHAT IS A HABIT?

**Habit ['habət]**

noun

*a settled tendency or usual manner of behavior;*

*an acquired mode of behavior that has become nearly or completely involuntary;*

*a behavior pattern acquired by frequent repetition or physiologic exposure that shows itself in regularity or increased facility of performance.*[15]

It can take anywhere from 18 to 254 days for a person to form a new habit and an average of 66 days for a new behavior to become automatic.[16]

1. Cameron, "The Industrial Revolution," https://staysafeapp.com/en-us/history-of-workplace-health-and-safety/
2. https://safetylineloneworker.com/blog/history-of-workplace-safety?rq=history
3. Cameron, "Factory Act," in "The Industrial Revolution."
4. Cameron, "Inspectors," in "The Industrial Revolution."
5. "Commonly Used Statistics, paragraph 1, https://www.osha.gov/data/commonstats
6. Cameron, "The introduction of 'duty of care' 1837," in "The Industrial Revolution."
7. Cameron, "Safety regulations increase," in "The Industrial Revolution."
8. Cameron, "Employer's Liability Act," in "The Industrial Revolution."
9. Cameron, "Continued Increase," in "The Industrial Revolution."
10. MacLaury, "Job Safety Law," https://www.dol.gov/general/aboutdol/history/osha
11. https://www.nixonlibrary.gov/president/executive-orders
12. OSHA, "Establishment Search."
13. OSHA, "Establishment Search."
14. UE NEWS, https://www.ueunion.org/stwd_safetyblame.html, Paragraph 9.
15. Merriam-Webster.com Dictionary, "habit."
16. Lally, van Jaarsveld, Potts, and Wardle.

## HABIT #1
# STOP MAKING SAFETY A PRIORITY

I first heard this concept from two company trainers with Kellogg, Brown & Root in Baghdad, Iraq.[17] They asked the class this question: "Should safety be a priority?" And, of course, everyone in the room replied with a resounding "YES." Everyone in the class was thinking, "If it's not a priority, I don't think I want to work for this company anymore." But the instructors looked at all of us and said, "Safety should never be a priority." I almost walked out, but I'm glad I didn't. Here is how they explained it to us:

Let's say you have to be at work at 8:00 a.m. every morning and, just for this exercise, let's say you have to drive 30 minutes from your house to your work location. So, to be on time, you must leave by 7:30 a.m. What time would you set your alarm to go off in the morning in order to wake up and be at work by 8:00? Some say 6:00 a.m. Others say anything from 7:00 a.m. (for the late sleepers) all the way to 4:00 a.m. (for those like me who need time to wake up first). But then, the question becomes "Why?" Why wake up at 6:00 in the morning when you only have a 30-minute drive and don't have to be there until 8:00? What is the extra 1½ hours for? When I ask this, I usually get answers like "I need coffee when I wake up." Or, "I must take a shower before I can start my day." Or, "I like to leave early just in case there's bad traffic." We could keep going, but you can fill in your own answers here. Why do you wake up before the time you have to leave to make it to work on time?

Written by Rod Courtney

Now let's say that today, right before you leave work, your boss approaches you and says, "The company CEO is having a meeting in the morning at 8:00 in the main conference room and you have to be there." This is one of those meetings that we all dread. The CEO is a stickler about punctuality, so if you are not sitting in the conference room at 7:59, you might as well pack up your stuff because you no longer have a job. (I know that's a bit extreme, but work with me here.) So, tonight, you go home and when it comes time to get in bed, you set your alarm for 6:00. But by accident you hit "p.m." instead of "a.m." Or you use your phone as an alarm and it does a forced IOS update in the middle of the night and wipes out all your alarms. The point is, for whatever reason, you overslept; we've all done it. You wake up and look at the clock and it says 7:25 a.m. **Oh no, I'm going to be late**! So you jump out of bed and then what? Do you still make breakfast? NO. Do you still take a shower? NO. Do you still make coffee or anything else that's not absolutely necessary? Of course not; you get in your vehicle as quickly as you can and you start driving. I'd be willing to bet that most of us would break a couple of traffic laws on the way there. I know I've done it. But what is the one thing, the only thing, that none of us would ever leave the house before we do? You will not walk out your door until you do *this*?

Some of you nailed it already and some of you are running through everything you have ever done in the morning trying to figure out what on earth I could be talking about. Let me ask you this: Have you ever been so late for something that you showed up naked? In a bad dream, maybe. But not in real life. That just doesn't make sense to us. We would never even think about doing something like that. We will always get dressed before we go anywhere. In fact, there are people in the United States that die in house fires every year, because they try to get dressed before they leave a burning building. See, all those things we do every morning before we leave are called priorities. And priorities are, by design, adjustable. You adjust your priorities depending on what you are trying to accomplish in that given amount of time. But getting dressed is not a priority. Getting dressed is a VALUE. Values do not change. So, safety should never be considered a priority. Some of you are saying: "That's just a play on words; that's what we mean." But I beg to differ. It's a culture thing. So the first habit is to stop making safety a priority and make it a value. Refer to it as and treat it as a value in everything you do.

## WHAT DOES VALUE-DRIVEN SAFETY LOOK LIKE?

Every level of employee, from the most-senior leader to the newly hired worker, clearly understands what is expected. There are specific, demanding standards for each person in all major work activities. Without adequate standards, there can be no meaningful measurement, evaluation, correction, or commendation of performance.[18]

Value-driven safety is "when it's so ingrained into every activity that it becomes impossible to ignore. There is little talk of doing things the safe way and more talk of doing things the right way. This is reflected in performance appraisals, salary adjustments, and promotions."[19]

Leaders around the world increasingly recognize that a well-managed safety system provides an operational strategy to improve overall management. But, in recent years, a significant number of major organizations have discovered that applying the tools and techniques of good safety management gives them not only reduced injuries and illnesses, but also offers measurable improvements in efficiency, quality, and productivity. This means that the Safety Department will be involved early in the business process and throughout, until the completion of the project. Everything begins and ends with safety.[20]

The heart of safety management is measuring performance in quantifiable, objective terms. Leading companies constantly assess their processes to determine if they are adequately controlling risk. Although they include in their "safety" measurement after-the-fact consequences such as recordable rates and lost time rates, they do not rely solely on lagging indicators. When safety is truly a value above all else, you will be able to focus on the leading indicators and stop an accident before it happens.[21]

What are our leading indicators? Human Performance Tools, site visits by all levels of leadership, proper training for everything that we do, positive reinforcement, hazard Identification, hazard correction, safety committees, true leadership commitment, and enforcement of the safety policies and procedures.[22]

Over the course of this book, we will discuss in detail Human Performance and how the principles and concepts are applied. Figure 2 is a visual example of an event and how, when used correctly, it is possible to make it safe for your employees to fail.

## Swiss Cheese Model of Safety

*Hazard · Human Performance Tools · Latent Weaknesses or Gaps · Capacity · Harm*

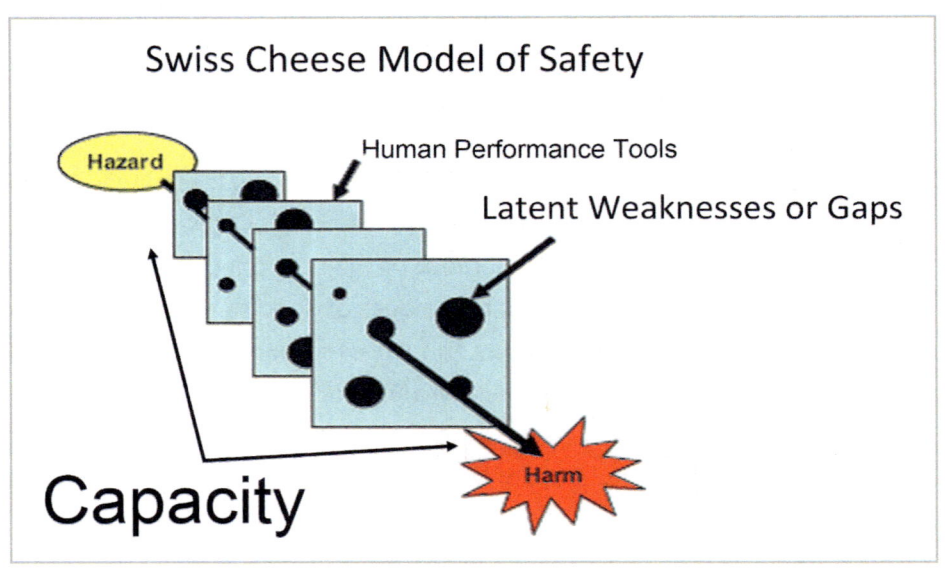

FIG 2 *Human Performance Tools at Work*[23]

The 8 Habits of a Highly Effective Safety Culture

17. Kellogg Brown & Root, LogCAP III Training Team (2003-2006).

18. Courtney, "Clearly Describe," in "Safety."

19. Courtney, "Make Safety," in "Safety."

20. Courtney, "Incorporate Safety," in "Safety."

21. Courtney, "Use Proactive Health and Safety Measures," in "Safety."

22. Ibid.

23. Adapted from https://mycontrolroom.com/human-factors-process-safety/

## HABIT #2

# MAKE IT SAFE FOR PEOPLE TO RAISE CONCERNS

In all the years I have been in the safety field, I have never heard anyone say, "If you report a safety concern, you're fired." They always say, "We want you to report everything." At least, that's what is said. But what is perceived by the employees? Always remember: right or wrong, perception is reality to the perceiver. So, what do the workers think will happen if they report a safety violation or a near miss or a minor accident? If you don't know, let me tell you. Too many times, employees believe that some sort of negative repercussion will happen if they report anything negative. If you don't believe me, do an anonymous survey of your employees and see for yourself. For those of you who are in or came from "the field" or worked "on your tools," you know exactly what I'm saying; you lived it.

So how do you create an environment where employees perceive they are safe bringing up concerns regarding safety?

Step one is to establish trust. What you don't want to do is come across like you are trying to sell something or that you have a hidden agenda, because all this will do is push them further away. So here is a list of seven practices you must do in order to establish trust:

Written by Rod Courtney

## 1. BE HONEST AND SUPPORT YOUR TEAM

Seems like a no-brainer, but remember it's based on their perception. So here are things you can do to build rapport with employee(s) and show them you are honest and supportive:

- Think before you speak.
- Say what you mean and mean what you say.
- Bend over backwards to communicate in an open and honest fashion.
- Simplify your statements so that everyone clearly understands your message.
- Tell it like it is, rather than sugarcoating it.
- Present both sides of each issue to engender objectivity.
- If you have a personal bias or a conflict of interest, make it known.
- Tell people the rationale behind your decisions so that your intent is understood.
- If something is misinterpreted, quickly correct the record.
- Don't shoot the messenger when someone tells you the truth. Thank them for their honesty and treat the information provided as a gift.
- Willingly accept responsibility by admitting a mistake or an error in judgment — in a timely fashion.
- Never compromise your integrity and reputation by associating yourself with people whose standards of integrity you mistrust.[24]

## 2. RESPOND CONSTRUCTIVELY TO PROBLEMS

This is an area that personally I had to work on. At first, I didn't realize that I was talking "at" people and not "to" them. Sometimes I didn't consider the years of experience and the type of experience I had, and would assume everyone else had the same. So, when I would try to coach or help my team out, it came across as very critical and not constructive. Here are a few things you can do to make sure you don't fall into that same trap:

- Use "I" messages instead of "You" messages.
- Communicate the entire message.
- Don't be defensive.
- Use specific language.
- Focus on the problem, not the person.
- Pay attention to your body language.

## 3. MAKE IT PERSONAL

At first, this may seem difficult, but it's actually one of the easiest to do. In the beginning, don't talk about work. Instead, talk about things that interest them. I'm a huge college football fan, so I can always find either another fan of the same team or, even better, a fan of a rival team. I like to have fun "talking smack" during football season. Even when my team is having a terrible year, I talk like they're going to win the championship. This tends to bring a sense of competition and camaraderie at the same time. But by discussing things that are important to them first, when you start to talk about safety concerns, they will be much more apt to continue to listen.

## 4. MODEL THE BEHAVIOR YOU WANT TO SEE

This is just the old adage to "lead by example." Here's something interesting: Every time you are observed breaking a safety rule, it ruins 30 days of safety talk. So, let's say you have a push on back injury safety and, for the next month, you discuss every possible back injury-related topic. Every day for 30 days, the discussion is about back safety. Then, you are observed on the 31st day lifting a box incorrectly or allowing someone else to lift incorrectly. You just negated the entire months' safety push on back injuries. The perception of the employees is "Well, if he/she doesn't take this seriously, then it must not be important." Remember, you are always on stage.

## 5. PROTECT YOUR EMPLOYEES

This can be interpreted in different ways. In this context, it means protecting them from unjust practices and reactions. We obviously want to protect everyone from the physical hazards but we also want to protect employees by standing up for them if they are treated unfairly. This happens more times that you may think, especially in a safety culture that is not entirely just. Later in the book, we will discuss just safety cultures and how to create them. But for now, please understand that none of this works in an unjust environment.

## 6. KEEP YOUR WORD

Many times, our word is all we have, and if you are known to go back on your promises, you will have a very hard time, not just in creating a successful safety culture, but in life in general. There will be times that you agree to something, and, for one reason or another, it just doesn't work out. But let this be the exception and not the norm. And, anytime you just can't keep a promise, be sure to communicate to the person or persons that are expecting you to come through.

And that leads us to the last thing on our list,

# 7. OVER-COMMUNICATE

In business, over communicating can be a bad thing, but, in safety and when trying to modify human behavior, you can't communicate enough. Please understand that I am not suggesting that you ramble on about every tiny detail. But when building trust, communication is something that you absolutely cannot overlook.

Building trust isn't something that usually happens overnight. It takes some time, but if you are sincere, trust and respect will come.

The last thing we must remember when building trust is that you are not just asking them to trust you, you're asking them to trust the company and sometimes that can be much more difficult. Here is a technique I learned over the years. I call it "convince the mascot." Every jobsite, every company, every group of people has a "mascot." The mascot is usually the person who has the dominant "Type-A" personality but is not pushy and domineering. They tend to talk more than most and have no problem asking questions during a meeting. You can usually pick the mascot out before you even introduce yourself to a group of people by simply standing back and watching them. The mascot is the one telling all the stories or teaching the underclassmen. They are the ones who everyone seems to gravitate to and wants to follow. If you can find the mascot, all you have to do is convince them to trust you (or the company) and they will convince the others. This technique can be used in many different applications but trying to get a large group to not only do the right thing, but rather *want* to do the right thing can be difficult. Find the mascot, convince them and just step back and watch.

When I came home from Iraq in 2006, I made a conscious decision to focus my career on the electrical power industry. I started working in renewable energy and built wind farms and solar plants all over the country. Early on,

I found myself working in West Texas for a company that had around 50% Danish employees. Similar to working in Iraq, there were some significant cultural safety differences between the employees from Denmark and those from the United States. It was a struggle to ask the entire project site to adhere to any rule and only half would even try. It's not that the Danish employees were being belligerent, they just did what they had always done and it was quite different from what OSHA requires.

One day, I noticed there was one Danish employee in particular that was the center of attention in most conversations. He told jokes and stories that really engaged those around him. I decided to get to know him better and see if I could use his influence to my advantage. Sure enough, after a week or two of learning all about his family back home, his dog named "Wag" and the 1968 Chevrolet Camaro he was trying to buy, I was able to convince him that these safety rules were not just to keep us in compliance with the federal regulations, but they were about making sure every employee went home at the end of the day the same way they showed up that morning, only a little wealthier.

The results were astonishing. In no time, he had helped convince half of the project site that working safely was the right thing to do. And from that time on, I rarely had to ask twice.

Once trust is established, you, your company and your employees need to have a complete paradigm shift and start to celebrate the reporting of near misses/great catches instead of making them punitive. This is thinking about safety differently, and for many, it is not going to feel right at first. But what we all must understand is that incidents **are** happening, even if they are not being reported. Studies show that, on average, a person will make 3-6 errors per hour.[25]

Let's be honest, most of those errors never amount to anything. Last week, I was on a business trip to California and was using my smartphone as a GPS.

A couple of miles before my next turn, my wife calls. I answered it hands-free (via Bluetooth). I heard the "Google Maps Lady" tell me to prepare to turn right in two miles, one mile, half of a mile . . . etc. yet I still missed my turn. We've all done that or something similar. Minor? Yes. Did it amount to anything? Not really, just a couple miles of driving. My point is that people make mistakes and we will never be able to stop them from happening.

So, let's take an office or project site and say there are ten employees working. That's at least thirty errors every hour and 240 over an eight-hour workday. You can't tell me that at least two or three of those do not meet the definition of a near miss: "An unplanned event that did not result in injury, illness or damage – but had the potential to do so."[26] Let's just say this number is 1/240, meaning that one near miss happens on every worksite every day. How would your company leadership or your client react if you reported five near misses every week? From experience, I can tell you that most would lose their minds and start trying to find someone to blame. But, like I said, this is safety *differently*, and our paradigm shift has taught us that we should be celebrating these reports. I've gone so far as to incentivize them. We've given money away for reporting near misses. Once I explained the following to my company and to our clients, it made perfect sense, and they no longer hold near misses against us on our scorecards.

Let's say one construction project site started reporting all incidents, because they felt the duty to do it and felt safe enough to do it. Every day for the next five days, this site reported near misses and work observations like improper hand placement, improper gloves, no gloves . . . all having to do with hand safety. When this information is put into a tracking database, or even an Excel spreadsheet, reports can be run and graphs created that will give an employer the ability to see all of the data over any given period of time. So when employees start reporting these things, the "hand injury" line of the graph will start to go up. And when it does, someone is about to have a hand injury. I don't know when or where, but it's about to happen. I can remember when Behavior-Based Safety (BBS) became the latest and

Written by Rod Courtney

greatest thing and we would hand out observation cards every day to different employees. At the end of the day they would bring the completed cards back to me and I would review the information. But then, what happened to the cards? Guess. Yep, they ended up in a box under my desk, and when the box filled up, the cards went in the trash. Some good information went in the garbage because we didn't track it. If you are going to collect data—and you absolutely need to in order to run an effective program—you have to track it. When the information is tracked correctly, it can be trended and you can see accidents before they happen.

In Figure 3 (page 40), you can see that once everyone buys into the fact that reporting all incidents is a positive thing (paradigm shift) and the data is tracked, trends can be seen in the information. When those trends are seen, you can focus on the leading indicators of that type of injury, get the information out to the jobsite and that trend line comes right back down. You just avoided an accident! And it's all because you made it truly safe for employees to raise concerns regarding safety.

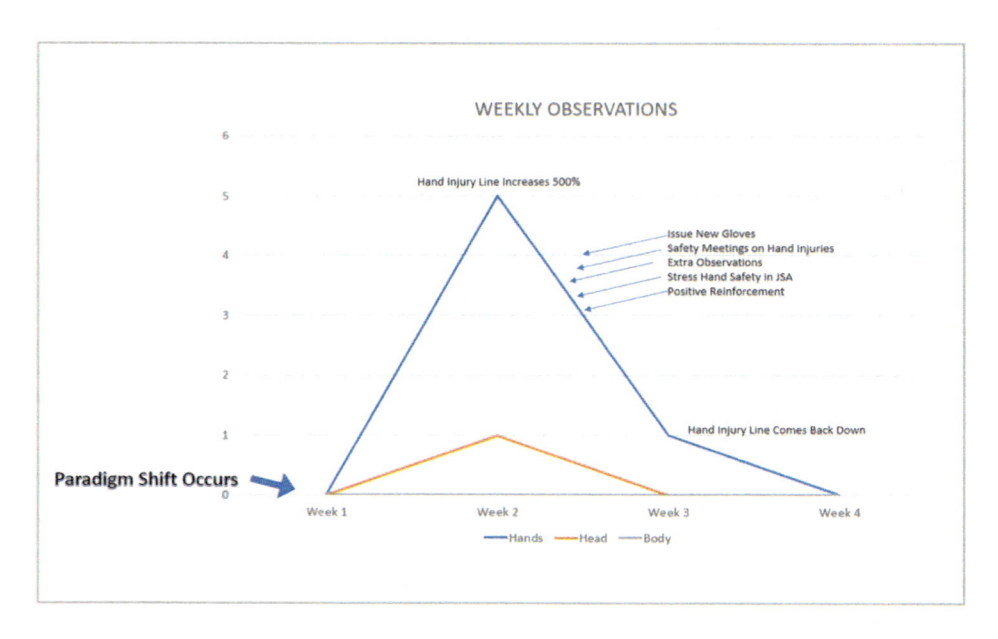

*FIG – 3 Tracking and Trending Near Miss Information*

The 8 Habits of a Highly Effective Safety Culture

24. Sonnenberg, "Honesty."
25. Thomson, "Why Tolerate."
26. Wikipedia contributors, "Near miss."

## HABIT #3

# MAKE SAFETY THE RESPONSIBILITY OF OPERATIONS

My very first job in safety was in 1997 with a small scaffolding company in Baton Rouge, LA. Like most people, at that point in my career I could spell O.S.H.A. but that's about all I knew about it. I was naïve and just followed the lead of those appointed above me. Understand that, back then, the larger companies—think Dow, DuPont, 3M, Exxon— were deep into behavior-based safety programs and trying to identify the unsafe conditions and unsafe acts caused by employees, but the smaller companies were still just winging it and I was well trained to be a "Safety Cop." Go out and find the employees doing something wrong and, as long as it doesn't affect our schedule or cost too much money, fix it. I had the authority to fire employees, as long as they weren't related to someone high up in the company. Looking back, I see now just how dysfunctional and counterproductive this was, but we all had to start somewhere.

Since most of my time was spent "being visible" for the customer in the field and turning a blind eye to anything that wasn't Immediately Dangerous to Life or Health (IDLH), I had plenty of free time to be the keeper and distributor of all Personal Protective Equipment (PPE), attend/perform most Job Safety Analyses (JSAs), perform and document all safety meetings and be the back-up forklift operator. Pretty much doing everything a Safety

Written by Rod Courtney

Professional should not be doing. It was 6-7 years later before I even heard about the concept of a value-driven, operationally based H&S program. So I learned some pretty bad habits early on.

I say this not to throw anyone under the bus or to try to say we should have been doing it differently all along. The truth is that we needed this window in time to be able to get to where we are today. I have been very fortunate to be able to speak at many events and I try to explain it like this: I am a former Army Combat Medic and I went to basic training at Fort Sill, OK. For me, during those eight weeks of boot camp, if it could go wrong, it probably did go wrong. I was out of shape and not mentally strong, so I became somewhat of a pet project for some of my drill instructors. Which basically means I got screamed at and did more pushups, flutter kicks and sit ups than anyone else in my battery. I hated every minute of it and thought about quitting every single day. But I had a dear friend who had gone through basic training just a few months before me, and he told me, "It's all a game. Their job is to break you down and rebuild you into a soldier. So, whatever you do, just don't quit." So I didn't. And while these were eight weeks of pure hell, I needed that to become who I am today. Just like all of the past safety mentalities (or lack thereof), we needed those times to be able to get where we are today.

So, if a safety professional isn't supposed to be in charge of PPE and everything that has the word "safety" in it, then what are we supposed to do? Well, here it is:

- Monitor
- Audit
- Review
- Advise

We said earlier that safety is better served when it is so ingrained into every activity that it becomes impossible to ignore. There is little talk of doing things the safe way and more talk of doing things the right way. In order to accomplish either of these, we must first understand that the safety of employees is a responsibility of Operations. This means that while we (the safety department) do develop and maintain the program, its implementation is owned by the people who it's designed to protect. Now, I am absolutely not saying that we as Safety Professionals should not correct unsafe behaviors, especially if they are IDLH, but that is a responsibility everyone on the project shares. It's called "Stop Work Authority." [27] I'm sure you've heard those words before. Every new-hire orientation talks about the employee's responsibility to 1) refuse to do work that is unsafe and 2) stop any job that is being done unsafely. So in that respect, correcting a safety violation is part of everyone's job, or at least it should be.

Let's say you are out for a stroll around your site and you come across someone doing something unsafe. You have two options here: 1) make them comply or 2) make them *want* to comply. More times than not, people will do as you tell them just out of respect for your title, but what good is temporary compliance just to appease you? The idea is to make them want to do it, and throughout my career, I have found three surefire ways to make someone actually want to do something.

## 1. MAKE 'EM LAUGH.

I have found that laughter can not only heal a person from the inside, but it can also change the way they see things. Let's say you are out on that jobsite stroll again and you see someone breaking a safety rule. Get your phone out and find some of the funny memes out there having to do with the violation you observed. Here are a few examples:

Someone with their hands or feet in a pinch point or near a machine guard. Show them this and say "When I see you with your hands there, this is all I can see."

Written by Rod Courtney

*These could be used in so many situations.*[28]

The idea is just to get them to laugh at themselves. Many times, this simple method will change the way someone behaves.

## 2. MAKE 'EM CRY.

I don't mean make them literally start sobbing. What I mean is "touch a nerve." Make it personal. Ask them about their children, their wife, their parents. Anyone who they love and who loves them. One time, I was using this one and the employee was in his mid-fifties and never had children. His wife left him because he worked too much and both his parents were deceased. So we talked about his new fishing boat. Not exactly the same effect, but it worked.

When you have an employee who you know has children or grandchildren, that is a perfect opportunity to ask for their names. Let's say the employee responds back with, "Well, I have a son named Bradley and a newborn daughter named Lillian (but we call her Lily)." Now you discuss with him how Bradley and Lily would feel if Dad didn't come home today. "What will they think when they see Mom crying and that big box being lowered into the ground?" Be sure to say the child's name; this makes it much more real to the person you are coaching.

Again, the point is to make it so personal that they stop and think about the repercussions of their actions. I've found this method to be really effective once I get to know the employee(s) and know their kids/grandkids/spouses' names already.

## 3. SHOCK 'EM.

Disclosure: This does not mean electrically shock your employees. Don't tell the OSHA investigator that Rod told you to hook your crews up to jumper cables in order to change their behaviors!

Written by Rod Courtney

Seriously, what I mean is tell them a story either about something that has happened directly to you or that you witnessed or that you heard about. It needs to be a story that really has a few "WOW" moments. One of my favorites is the story of Charlie Morecraft. Charlie was an operator at an Exxon plant in New Jersey and had a horrific accident. He tells his whole story on the video *Remember Charlie*. He had been asked to work some additional overtime and he agreed. During the night, he had to open a pipe flange and reroute the bioethanol hydrocarbon, which he says he "had done a thousand times before." He didn't do it the "correct" way but he did it the way he and everyone else had come to do it, by taking shortcuts. He goes on to say "When the flange opened, from somewhere in that pipeline—to this day I don't know where—a flood of hydrocarbons hit me square in the face and temporarily blinded me. I started running to the emergency shower when a spark caused the entire unit to blow, and I blew with it." Charlie describes the humiliation and pain like I've never heard before. The description of being debrided still makes me cringe. He says "every day, they would lower me into this large metal tank and scrub off the dead skin. But the live skin and the nerve endings "came with it."[29] When you hear this and similar stories, you walk away thinking, "My God, I never want anything like that to happen to me." And there are probably fifty others who do talks and have written books about their accidents and use their stories to try to keep others from making the same mistake. This method is by far the most time consuming, but once you get the hang of it, you can tell the story highlights in a safety meeting and just watch the reactions of those in attendance.

Sometimes you can use a combination of these, depending on what the employee responds to best. Do they learn from laughter or should you make it personal and touch a nerve or should you tell a true story about someone who was terribly injured doing the same or similar actions? It's up to you, but all you are trying to do is make someone "want" to do something versus "have" to do it.

Earlier, I mentioned the four main responsibilities of a Safety Professional in an operationally based H&S program. Let's look at each of them for a moment.

# MONITOR

This does not mean sit behind your computer monitor all day. In this context, we are talking about the verb "monitor."

> **mon·i·tor ['mänədər]**
> verb
>
> ............
>
> *observe and check the progress or quality of (something) over a period of time; keep under systematic review.*
>
> ............
>
> SIMILAR: observe, watch, keep an eye on, keep track of, track[30]

In order to be effective, you must know what's going on in your area. Maybe that's a job/project site or maybe it's a warehouse or a fabrication shop. Maybe it's an office or maybe it's a combination of all of these. But no matter what your area consists of, you can only be effective if you monitor all the activities going on. This means 1) Get to know the employees on a personal level and know their personality type, and 2) Be involved in the job planning so you will know what is going on at all times. Some companies have a "Three-week look ahead" meeting or a "Plan of the Day" (POD) meeting, after action reviews, pre-job briefings, etc. A forward-thinking Safety Professional will be involved in the meetings that discuss production, schedules, quality and costs. This way, you can stay one step ahead of the workload. You should monitor all current activities and be prepared for all future activities.

Let me be clear though, monitor does not equal "bird-dog." That means don't just stand and hover over an employee or a crew of employees. All this does is make them nervous, and it will be counterproductive. What I like to do is walk around and talk with employees about anything but safety. I talk about the football game last night or the fishing trip they were going on last weekend or the brisket I'm going to put on the smoker this weekend. The point is, monitor with your eyes and not your mouth. When you, "The

Written by Rod Courtney

Safety Guy/Gal," walk up, what do they expect you to talk about? Safety stuff. So, when you start talking about things that interest them, you accomplish a few things: 1) you are building a relationship, 2) you are making your presence less intimidating, and 3) you are building a relationship. Yes, I know I said that one twice, but it's the most important aspect. Because without a positive relationship, the rest will fail.

Notice I never said, "Don't correct unsafe behaviors," because this is still part of what we do. It's just using basic psychology to create an environment where employees feel safe with you around. So if you see it, you own it. If you see an unsafe condition, it is your responsibility to correct it or have it corrected. Never turn a blind eye. But it's "how" you make the correction that matters. We have to be firm, fair and consistent with our responses, but that doesn't mean you become a safety cop like I was trained to be in my early years. Remember, LAUGH – CRY – SHOCK.

# AUDIT

au·dit ['ôdət]
noun

*an official inspection of an individual's or organization's accounts, typically by an independent body.*

SIMILAR: inspect, examine, survey, look over, go over, go through.[31]

Auditing and monitoring go hand in hand. Auditing is the documentation of what you monitor. You have to give the operations side a true picture of how their project is progressing, but you also don't want to focus on lagging indicators. There is a balance we need to find where we can give the company leaders the information, and they need to make decisions without giving them a "grade." Remember being in school and you listened in class (most of the time) and you even studied your notes for homework (except when you were hanging out with your friends)? Then you took the test and knew without a doubt it wasn't going to be the best grade you ever had. But when the teacher gave you that test back and the grade was even lower than you imagined, how did that make you feel toward that teacher? My point is that we are not here to "write people up" or "grade" them. Your audit/inspection form and audit/inspection report should be two different things. One is for you to use as a guide to make sure everything gets checked and you can keep track of safe and unsafe conditions. The other is an executive summary-type report which can be easily understood and discusses everything you observed over that given period of time.

What I like to do with these reports involves another psychological technique. Its call the sandwich method. This is where you start off talking about the positive aspects of the inspection then go into the areas for improvement and always end it with another positive note or one last thing you saw that was safe/done well. This method sandwiches the corrective actions needed between two aspects of the job that are going very well, and, as crazy as it may sound, it makes the delivery much more palatable. Remember, we are not trying to tell anyone how wrong they are. We only want to inform operations of their gaps and give them solutions to fix them.

# REVIEW

**re·view ['rə'vyoō]**
noun

*a formal assessment or examination of something with the possibility or intention of instituting change if necessary.*

SIMILAR: analysis, evaluation, assessment, appraisal, examination, investigation, scrutiny, inquiry, exploration, probe, inspection.[32]

In this context, review means reviewing company policies to ensure compliance with regulatory agencies. The way I like to do this is to get others involved and help them become a subject matter expert about a particular section of our policy manual and allow them to recommend the change. This gives employees some extra knowledge that they otherwise would not have received and it allows them to feel like a part of the program. I've used safety committees for this, and it worked out great. I've also given sections of the safety manual to different Safety Professionals throughout my company and allowed them to learn the subject(s) and recommend changes. Either way, we have to ensure our written policies are always up to date. And if you can get some employee involvement at the same time, why not?

## ADVISE

**ad·vise ['əd'vīz]**
verb

*offer suggestions about the best course of action to someone.*

SIMILAR: counsel, give counsel, give counseling, give guidance, guide.[33]

Years ago, I had a sign hanging on the door to my office that read, "If you enter this office with a problem, bring a solution with you." The Operations team has enough to focus on without us adding to the chaos. So, when you find gaps or areas that need attention, always give them at least one option to fix it. Advise them on how to maintain compliance and advise them on the repercussions if they choose not to.

28. OSHA SEC. 5 (a) (1)

29. Morecraft, Remember Charlie.

30. Merriam-Webster.com Dictionary, "monitor."

31. Merriam-Webster.com Dictionary, "audit."

32. Merriam-Webster.com Dictionary, "review."

33. Merriam-Webster.com Dictionary, "advise."

### HABIT #4
# FOCUS LEFT OF ZERO

The best way to visualize this concept is to picture a number line with a zero right in the middle. Everything on the right side of zero are things we have no control over (i.e. accidents, environmental incidents, safety violations). I'm sure some of you are saying, "But if we discipline employees, the safety violations will stop." No, they won't; employees will just get better at hiding them. But to the right side of zero are all things that have already happened. You can't go back in time and change them, so don't focus your energy there. On the "Left-of-Zero," you see the things you can control (i.e. human performance training and tools, safety meetings, pre-job briefings, near miss reporting) and when we put more focus on what we can control vs. what we can't, amazing things happen.

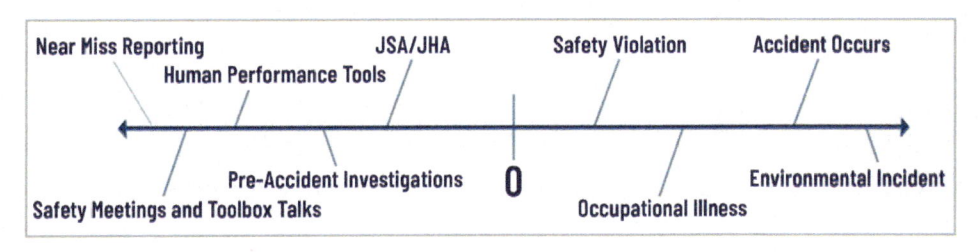

FIG – 4 Left of Zero Timeline

For years, this has been referred to as leading and lagging indicators, and while, technically, they still are, it's a way we can actually visualize where we should focus.

Written by Rod Courtney

So why should we focus left of zero? Because human nature will drag us down if we don't. Think about it like this:

You're an Olympic runner and your race is the 100-meter sprint. You've been running since you were a child; you were All District and All State in High School. You went to college on a full scholarship and broke every school record. Now here you are in front of a crowd of 100,000+ and you are representing your country as an Olympic athlete. You walk out on the track and the crowd goes crazy cheering for you. You stretch for a minute with the other runners and then get into the starting blocks. Where are you focused? Some will say "I'm focused on the sound of that starting pistol;" others, "I'm focused on the finish line." But when world-class sprinters are asked, they say, "I'm focused 10 meters beyond the finish line."

Human nature is to slow down right before we finish something. Don't believe me? Next time you climb a flight of stairs, carefully "trot" to the top. What will happen? More than likely, you'll unconsciously slow down two steps before the top. We all do it. And if you are about to run the race of your life and you focus on anything but beyond the finish line, chances are you'll slow down a split second before you finish.

So we as humans need to focus beyond where we want to be, so we can finish strong and not let our nature cause us to fail.

Now that we know where to focus our attention, what information do we track? All construction companies are scored by their clients and potential clients by two basic metrics.

- Workers Compensation Experience Modification Rate (EMR)
- OSHA 300 log information (TRIR, DART...)

If your EMR goes above a 1.0, then many companies will not even allow you to bid on a project. What does a 1.0 EMR mean? Well, simply put, it is based off the number and amount of workers comp claims from the previous years. 1.0 is considered average, anything below 1.0 is better than average and anything above is considered worse than average. Many companies are getting away from using this metric as a hard qualifying factor because this number can be manipulated. All a company has to do is the same thing any of us do with an insurance claim; if the deductible is cheaper than the repairs, we pay it out of pocket. If someone has had too many claims on their insurance, what happens? Their insurance rates go up. So employers would rather pay medical costs out of pocket rather than turning it over to insurance, because when they pay out of pocket, their EMR isn't affected.

OSHA recordkeeping is quite a bit different. There is a law that says employers SHALL record certain injuries and illnesses and if an employer chooses to violate those regulations, they face anything from fines to prison time. So any incident that required "medical treatment" has to be placed on a log. At the end of the year, companies take the number of incidents and multiply it by 200,000 and divide that by the total man-hours for the company. That gives a company their Total Recordable Incident Rate (TRIR). It's the same formula for every company in every industry, but construction companies specifically rely on the results to stay in business. The rate is then compared to the average rate for your North American Industrial Classification System (NAICS) number. The NAICS assigns a number to every industry and most subindustries.[34]

Example:
ABC Construction Inc. does work on "oil and gas pipeline and related structures" and their NAICS is 23712.[35]

The Bureau of Labor Statistics (BLS) puts out the annual average incident rates per NAICS number and the average for their industry is 0.6. Which translated to 0.6 of an accident for every 100 employees.

In 2021, ABC Construction had three recordable incidents and worked 987,654 total man hours.

$$3 \times 200{,}000 = 600{,}000$$
$$600{,}000 / 987{,}654 = \mathbf{0.6}$$

So, ABC had to work nearly a million man-hours in order to be *average* with 3 recordable accidents.[36]

But the whole point of the Left of Zero concept is to stop focusing on the things you can't control and focus more on the things you can. While EMRs and TRIRs have to be calculated each year and should be tracked, we should focus more effort on things like:

- Training completed
- Near misses reported
- Safety meetings completed
- Job safety analyses completed
- Work observations
- Human Performance traps identified
- Organizational weaknesses identified/corrected

By tracking this type of data, you will be able to see trends and get ahead of an accident. Yes, you will be able to see into the future and stop an accident before it even happens.

Here's what happens if we take the number of near misses reported and track/trend the data.

Let's go back to the industrial job site and use the same example from Habit #2. We are going to track and trend all near misses reported. Once we have a culture that feels safe reporting issues regarding safety (which can require a substantial paradigm shift, but it's necessary), we can really make a huge impact. For the next week, you receive one near miss report every day from the field crews. The items identified in each are as follows:

- Improper hand placement
- Not wearing gloves when required
- Left hand in a pinch point near machine guard
- Improper gloves for the task
- Carpenter helper's finger nearly hit by a hammer

Now, when you put all that information into a tracking system, you will see the "hand injury" line start to go up on a line graph. Now you know that employees are about to have a hand injury. You don't know when or where, but I assure you it's about to happen.

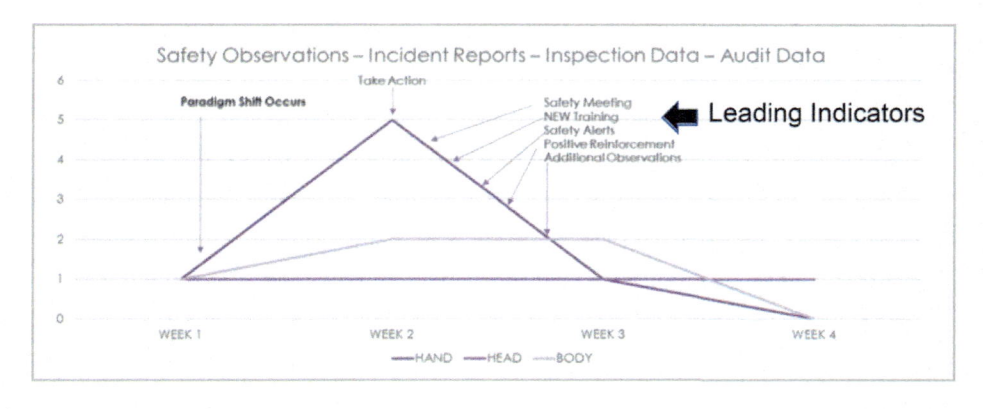

FIG – 5 Applying Leading Indicators to Keep an Accident from Occurring

Written by Rod Courtney

So, over the following week, you address hand injuries in your safety meetings. You make sure everyone has been trained on the use of equipment and understands the pinch points; you send out a safety alert to all sites discussing hand injuries; every time you see an employee wearing gloves and protecting their hands, you reinforce the positive behavior; you even go so far as to, for one afternoon, assign an employee to walk around and do nothing but look for possible hand injury causes. Once you do all of this, what do you think happens to that hand injury line on the graph? It goes right back down again. You just avoided an accident! Now, be sure to give praise when its due and thank everyone for the extra focus, because next week it'll be something else and you'll again need them to report every near miss. Before you know it, you're getting 2-3 reported each day, and the more data you put into your tracking system, the further into the future you can see. And by focusing Left-of-Zero, you are able to duplicate these results over and over. My whole career—and I'm sure yours as well—we have been told "don't focus on the lagging indicators." Yet it is impossible to track something that hasn't happened, so in that sense, everything we track is a lagging indication, right? Well, sort of. See, Habit #4 Focus Left of Zero and Habit #2 Make it Safe for People to Raise Concerns go hand in hand. One cannot exist without the other. A "Just" safety culture must be created before employees will report the information you need so you can track it and then implement leading indicators.

In Todd Conklin's book, *Pre-Accident Investigation*, there is an exercise you can do in an office environment, warehouse, construction site—pretty much anywhere—with employees. Get some 3x5 cards and some pencils. Pass them out to everyone in the meeting and explain that you have 2 questions to ask but everyone only gets 30 seconds to answer each one. Get a stopwatch and ask this question first: *"If an injury were to happen here in the next week, what kind of injury would it be?"* After 30 seconds, everyone stops writing. Then ask, *"If that injury did happen at this location, where would it most likely happen"?*[37] This is not an exercise you can do very often, but once a year is plenty to get some great information and show you where "Left of Zero" is.

So, track all data, leading and lagging indicators. The leading indicators will show you what is working best on any particular site/office. The lagging indicators will show you where you are about to have an accident. Now, implement the leading indicators that have been shown to work best for your organization and watch that negative trend line (Fig 5) come back down. You just avoided an accident.

34. U.S. Bureau of Labor Statistics, "Injuries."
35. Ibid.
36. OSHA, "Clarification."
37. Conklin 2012.

## HABIT #5
# STOP MANAGING PEOPLE

Over the years, I have experienced some of the absolute best and absolute worst "managers" in the world. I'm sure you have come across both types as well. Here is the conclusion I have come to: *"You cannot manage people. You manage situations and you have to lead people."*

One of the best leadership courses on the planet is the US Army Ranger School. The purpose of the Army's Ranger course is to prepare these Army volunteers—both officers and enlisted Soldiers—in combat arms-related functional skills. The Rangers' primary mission is to engage in close combat and direct-fire battles.

The Ranger Course was conceived during the Korean War and was known as the Ranger Training Command. The Ranger Training Command was inactivated and became the Ranger Department, a branch of the Infantry School at Fort Benning, GA, on October 10, 1951. Its purpose was, and still is, to develop combat skills of selected officers and enlisted personnel. This requires them to perform effectively as small-unit leaders in a realistic, tactical environment, and under mental and physical stress; approaches that are found in actual combat. Emphasis is placed on the development of individual combat skills and abilities through the application of the principles of leadership, while further developing military skills in the planning and conduct of dismounted infantry, airborne, airmobile, amphibious independent squad, and platoon-size operations. Graduates return to their units to

Written by Rod Courtney

pass on these skills. While most will never enlist in the military, much less volunteer for Ranger school, the leadership principles still apply.[38]

## IF YOU FAIL TO MAKE A GREAT PLAN, YOU CAN PLAN ON FAILING.

Some of the best planners in the world are US military generals. They have the knowledge, training and experience to plan a battle down to the minute. But, as they will all tell you, that plan goes out the window as soon as the first round is fired. So a good plan has the ability to change when it's necessary but can still achieve the objective.

## LEADERSHIP IS NOT ABOUT RANK OR TITLE; IT IS ABOUT INSPIRING THE PEOPLE BESIDE YOU.

Think for just one minute about who you believe is/was the best leader(s) in the world. Not just in the military, but in your current company or maybe a past employer. But who was the best leader you've ever seen or heard of? I promise you that person understood better than anyone that he/she didn't have all the answers. The best leaders surround themselves with people smarter than they are and allow them to make decisions based on their expertise. Here is a list of a few of the best leaders in history:

- Mahatma Gandhi (1869–1948)
- Nelson Mandela (1918–2013)
- Winston Churchill (1874–1965)
- Martin Luther King, Jr. (1929–1968)
- Abraham Lincoln (1809–1865)
- Mother Teresa (1910–1997)
- George Washington (1732–1799)
- Dalai Lama (1935–present)
- Franklin D. Roosevelt (1882–1945)

This list is about as diverse as you can get when it comes to a list of people. But what is the one common denominator among each of them? They hired/appointed people and put them in positions to advise on their strengths. This process starts with you having the ability to inspire others.

I grew up in a small town in South Louisiana called Denham Springs. One of my best friends growing up was a guy named Jean-Paul Courville. To be honest, at this time in my life, I did just enough to get by. If I needed to pass a test or a class, I was happy with a "D." If one of my coaches had us running wind sprints, I gave about 50%-75% of my effort, just enough to keep from getting yelled at. The summer between my junior and senior year and Jean-Paul's sophomore and junior year, I didn't see J.P. at all. We didn't have cell phones back then and every time I called his house, his parents would tell me, "He's in the shed." What on earth does that mean, "**in the shed**"? Well, my focus that summer was making money and chasing girls (full disclosure: I didn't do very well at either). But when the fall of 1988 came round and it was time to go back to school, I saw J.P. for the first time in a little over three months. And HE WAS JACKED! I'm serious. A few months before, he was an average height, pudgy, low self-confidence high-school kid and now he looked like the Hulk. Come to find out, that summer, J.P. had asked his dad if he could join a gym and his dad told him he wouldn't pay for a membership unless he could prove he was serious. See, up to that point, J.P. was a lot like me and did just enough to get by and sticking with something to completion just wasn't a concern. Well, he made a commitment to go into his back yard in an old, dilapidated shed that had a weight bench, a couple of dumbbells, a pull-up bar and a couple hundred pounds of iron weights. So, when I would call and his mom or dad would tell me he was "in the shed," that meant he was out there getting after it. Working out 2-3 times a day, 6-7 days a week. And the transformation was astonishing.

The next year, I left Denham Springs and went into the Army. Jean-Paul enlisted in the Marine Corps the very next year. Our careers took us in different directions, so we didn't speak again for many years, until the invention of social media. When we finally reconnected, J.P. was a Gunnery Sgt (E-7) in the Marines and, shortly after, got promoted to E-8 (Master Gunnery Sgt). He had made a name for himself for not only being a poster-boy Marine but also a motivational speaker. He's been asked to speak at numerous events, both civilian and military, and one of his talks was about the difference between motivation and inspiration. Here is what he said: *"Motivation is like a cup of coffee. It might motivate someone, but after an hour or two the caffeine wears off and the motivation might wear off. But if you do it right and you inspire someone, that inspiration will last a lifetime."*[39]

## WHEN THINGS GO WRONG, DON'T STAND AROUND.

In the first principle above, we talked about planning and having a plan when that plan doesn't work; well, this principle falls right in line with that. Murphy's Law states that "if it can go wrong, it will go wrong"[40]; we just have to be prepared for it. One of the greatest skills I've learned throughout my career is to remain calm even in the most stressful situations. This is not something that comes naturally to anyone. It has to be practiced and perfected. But when things go wrong, and they will, calmly and deliberately make decisions to get everything back on track. When going through the Police Academy in Savannah, GA (Class 197-A), they taught us a way to practice and develop this skill. It's called the "What If" game. The idea is to look at your surroundings, find something that could go wrong and, in your mind, say, "What If?" Now, run through the steps in your head of how you would react. From beginning to end, what would you do and how would you do it?

Here's an example: Let's say we're at an office and about to have our quarterly company business review meeting. The conference room is all set up, there are donuts, granola bars, coffee, water and soft drinks laid out and everyone is starting to file in. In your mind, say, "What if there's a fire" or, "What if an earthquake were to occur right now; how would I respond?" Do this exercise often so when the time comes and it does happen, you will be able to make calm and calculated decisions to protect your life and the lives of those around you. I'm not suggesting you overthink it, just use the motto of the Boy Scouts of America: "Be Prepared."

## BELIEVE IN YOURSELF AND YOUR TEAM.

If we go back to the second principle, and you've been a good leader and put people into positions to help them and your department to succeed, then this one should be easy. But there is one thing that can hold you back. This was one of the hardest lessons for me to learn over the years. I did everything right. I became a student of communication, leadership and influence. I put people in positions where their expertise could make us successful, but I didn't allow them to shine. See, while we agreed on the end result, we didn't agree on the path to get there, and I had a hard time letting go of my way being the only way. The old adage "If you want something done right, you have to do it yourself" absolutely does not apply here. You and your team need to agree on the vision, but do not have to agree on the methods and means. So, believe in your team and let them shine.

## MAKE A DIFFERENCE.

This last principle taken from the US Army Ranger Handbook is purposefully very broad. The act of making a difference can change from one day to the next, even one minute to the next. So I am going to break this one down into a few different parts.[41, 42]

Master Sergeant Deantoni Littleton (aka @Dirtybirdfitness) has been an inspiration to so many and, when I asked him to help me define leadership, here is what he said: *"Leadership can be defined so many different ways. To be an effective leader, you first need to understand how to lead. Lead by actions, not just by words. Being a leader isn't just about a paycheck; there comes responsibilities as well. A leader doesn't hide behind their rank. A leader doesn't abuse their rank. A leader doesn't show favoritism. A leader is fair and impartial. A leader is a human being that never forgets where they came from. Be the leader that you would follow. Always take time to communicate if someone has a problem. Never give up on yourself or your Soldiers."*

In closing out this chapter and the fifth habit, "Stop Managing People," I want to discuss the essential qualities of a good leader.

Whether you're cultivating your leadership skills or hiring new managers, learning about what qualities make a good leader is essential.

While in the Army, I had the opportunity to work with some of the best and the absolutely worst leaders to ever wear the uniform. Toxic leadership is like a virus. Once it starts, it will infect every part of your organization and believe me, Motrin will not help!

Like many of you, I have reviewed hundreds of résumés and so many people list "I'm a natural born leader" as one of their skills. I'm sorry to disappoint you, but leaders are not born; they're developed. It's a skill like any other. It takes time and the calculated, deliberate intention of learning leadership skills. You can research leadership skills on the internet and you'll find everything from "Five Traits of Great Leader" to "Twenty-Five Traits of a Great Leader." And the fact is, they're all correct. Being a student of leadership is like being a Medical Doctor; methods, means, concepts and strategies are constantly changing and you have to be willing to change with them. Also, each "patient" is a little different. What works for one may not work for the other. So you have to understand your employees and know what makes them tick.

The best leaders do a few things consistently the same. The first of which is the ability to develop new leaders. We have all worked with someone that kept all pertinent information secured so that only they could access it and send it out when they felt it was necessary. I call this person "the keeper of all information." If someone is so insecure that they feel the need to create job security by not openly sharing all information, then they shouldn't be in a leadership position.

> *Developing leaders is a skill set in itself and I could write an entire book on this topic alone. But here is what you have to know: "If your actions inspire others to dream more, learn more, do more and become more, you are a leader."*
>
> -JOHN QUINCY ADAMS

I have been asked before, "What type of person makes the best leader?" and I always say, "The ones who have failed the most." I am who I am and where I am today only because I have failed more than most of you. So, learn how to handle failure. "Failure is a part of life. How you handle it as a leader speaks volumes to your employees. Anger and finger pointing is always counterproductive. Instead, if you want to know how to be a great leader, explore with your team what went wrong and how things could have been done differently to ensure success. Take responsibility for any part you played in the missed goal. Together, identify things that can be improved going forward. And hold employees accountable as needed — with grace."[43]

40. Army Ranger Training Brigade, "History" Paragraph 1.
41. Gaynor, "Motivation."
42. Wikipedia contributors, "Murphy's Law."
43. OUOnline staff, "8 Ways."

Written by Rod Courtney

HABIT #6

# STOP TRYING TO FIX THE WORKER

In chapter one, we talked briefly about the origin of Behavior-Based Safety (BBS). An insurance investigator named H.W. Heinrich studied the cause of workplace accidents and concluded that 88% were caused by "Unsafe Acts." Years later, this information became the foundation of BBS.

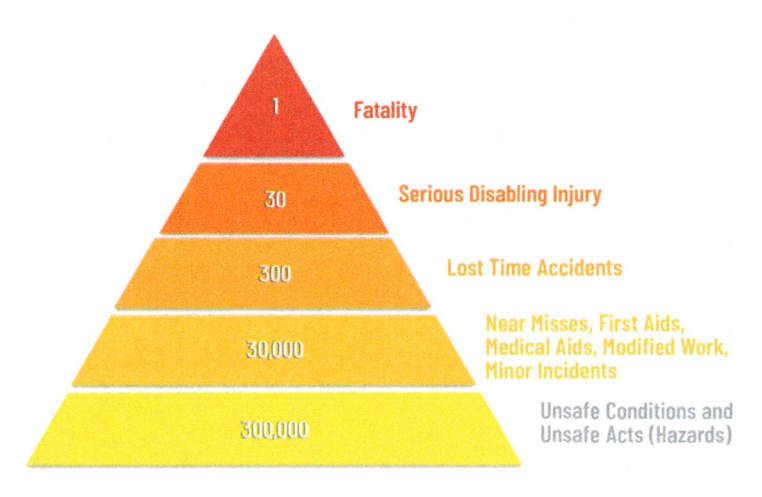

```
        1      Fatality
       30      Serious Disabling Injury
      300      Lost Time Accidents
    30,000     Near Misses, First Aids,
               Medical Aids, Modified Work,
               Minor Incidents
   300,000     Unsafe Conditions and
               Unsafe Acts (Hazards)
```

FIG 6 – Heinrich Triangle

This theory has some truth to it. If all unsafe acts can be eliminated, then he is correct; we could also eliminate all minor incidents, major incidents, serious injuries and fatalities. But… [There's always a "but," isn't there?] But is it possible to eliminate unsafe acts? Not as long as humans are involved. People make mistakes and no matter how hard they try, they always will.

Written by Rod Courtney

When eliminating hazards, we use the hierarchy of controls. It starts with eliminating the hazard at the top of the inverted triangle and goes all the way down to providing protective equipment at the tip (which should always be the last resort).[44]

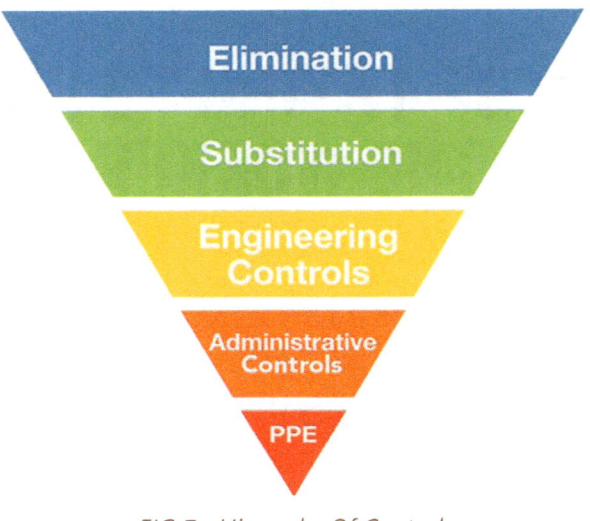

*FIG 7 - Hierarchy Of Controls*

"Elimination" would mean the hazards no longer exist. You have eliminated them and therefore none of the other control hierarchies even matter. But all unsafe conditions cannot and will not ever be completely eliminated.

So what about unsafe behaviors? Is it possible to eliminate unsafe behaviors? Absolutely not. Not as long as humans are involved, that is.

And as it turns out, while Mr. Heinrich meant well and his theory helped us get to where we are today, a little research will show that he did in fact travel around the country and interview over a thousand companies, employers and employees about accidents that occurred at their workplace. But who exactly did he speak with? See, back in the 1930s when this study was done, most employees who were injured on the job were either fired or sent somewhere else to work because they were considered "unsafe." When Mr. Heinrich spoke with the companies about the accident(s), he spoke to the company managers and usually the injured employee's supervisor. What do you think they said when they were asked, "So, Mr. Supervisor/Ms. Manager, what happened in that accident involving Mr. Employee? What caused the accident?"

Even today, if an investigator were to come to most companies out there are ask the Supervisor or Manager of the injured employee, "What caused the accident?" they would be told it was the employee's fault. The employee didn't follow procedure. The employee wasn't paying attention to his surroundings. The employee knew better than to do it that way. And back in the 1930s, you can rest assured that's exactly what they did. See, it's human nature to find someone to blame. Any time an accident happens and an investigation occurs (especially if by an insurance agency or federal/state/local authority), their mindset is "Who is at fault? Who can we blame?" How many of the people interviewed by Mr. Heinrich told him it was a faulty policy or bad safety culture? My point is that there are a lot of holes in the whole BBS method of safety.

Today, we use a more "Human Performance" approach to safety. While some will say the term "Human Performance" is just another "buzzword" and just the "flavor or the month," it truly isn't. Human Performance is scalable, sustainable and the base off which all other programs are built.

Throughout this book we have mentioned the word "culture" numerous times. But what does "safety culture" even mean? Here is my definition: *"A safety culture is what the employees do when no one is watching."*

There are five basic principles to Human Performance.[45] If you start with these, your program will grow into something that creates a positive culture.

# ERROR IS NORMAL AND EVEN THE BEST PEOPLE MAKE MISTAKES.

Let me ask you this: at any time this week, have you typed out an email or a text? Most of us will answer with a resounding yes to that one. Now, while you were typing out those emails or texts, how many times did you have to hit the backspace button? See, each time you did, it was because of an error. Mind you, these are extremely minor and rarely cause any real issues. That is, unless you hit "send" without checking what you wrote.

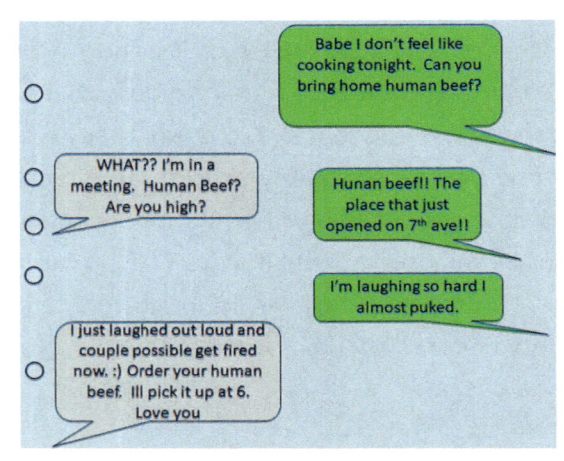

*FIG-8 Auto Correct*

*FIG-9 Auto Correct*

74   The 8 Habits of a Highly Effective Safety Culture

Then it could be a problem. The two examples above are funny, but imagine if you had sent one of these to a new potential client.[46]

No matter if you work in an office, a warehouse, a factory or a construction site, you make errors every hour of the day and so does every other employee. So, your error might be a funny autocorrected text or email, while an electrician on a construction site is making the same number of errors, on average, as everyone else, but these errors have the potential to be catastrophic.

Before we can move on with the next four principles, you have to understand principle number one: People make mistakes and no matter how hard we try, no matter how many BBS observation cards we do or how much training or retraining we do, they always will.

## BLAME FIXES NOTHING.

We mentioned earlier that it is human nature to find someone to blame when something goes wrong. In order to create a truly just and sustainable safety culture, we have to make a very conscious effort to stop doing it. After studying Human and Organizational Performance and listening to or reading the words of some of the best in the business, I still have to remind myself that, unless the act was culpable, then blaming someone is going to be counterproductive.

Let me be clear: I am not saying there should be no repercussions for acts that are found to be intentional violations. There is a difference between Accountability and Culpability.

> **Accountability**
> 
> noun
> 
> *the fact or condition of being accountable; responsibility.*[47]

**Culpability**

noun

*responsibility for a fault or wrong; blameworthiness.*[48]

What happens when we blame someone for an error/mistake?

**Human Error** → Individual counseled and/or disciplined → Reduced trust → Less communication → Management less aware of jobsite conditions → Latent organizational weaknesses persist → More flawed defenses and error precursors → (back to Human Error)

**BLAME CYCLE**

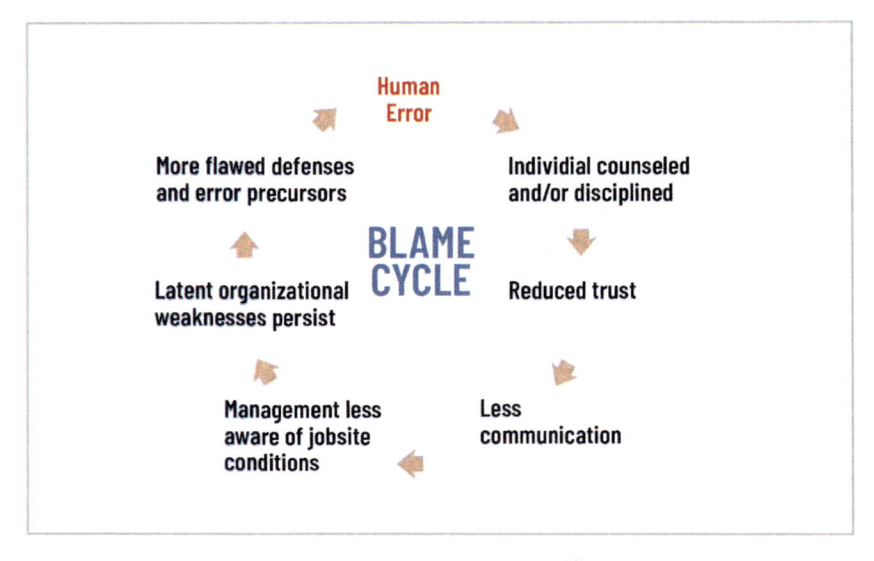

*FIG-10 The Blame Cycle*[49]

An honest mistake occurs and historically, here's how we approach it:

- Counsel or discipline the employee,
- Which causes trust to be diminished,
- Which causes communication between workers and leadership to be negatively affected,
- Which makes management less aware of the jobsite conditions.
- This, in turn, allows the latent organizational weaknesses to continue,
- And flawed defenses and error precursors also continue.

And the cycle will continue.

We have to break this cycle at the beginning. When errors occur, do not blame anyone. Todd Conklin said it best when he said, "When an incident occurs, you have two options, get better or get even, but you can't do both."[50]

We should be celebrating the reporting of minor incidents and near misses, not blaming and causing discontent.

A few years ago, I attended a conference where T. Shane Bush, the co-founder of BushCo HPI, Inc., did a presentation based on the Department of Energy (DOE) Human Performance Handbooks. Mr. Bush is another Human Performance pioneer and very well respected in the industry. During his presentation, he discussed the "Just Culture Decision Tree."

When I'm discussing the blame cycle and employee discipline, one of the most asked questions I get is, "So you expect us to just stop holding employees accountable and disciplining them when they mess up?" The answer is, "It depends." The Just Culture Tree helps to determine culpability. And if an employee's actions were intentional or sabotage, then, yes, discipline is warranted.

This chart (page 74) provides instruction on the use of the Human Performance Just Culture Decision Tree. It is a proven management tool intended to help determine the culpability level of an individual in response to events or near misses triggered by human error. When used in conjunction with accountability, the tool supports the fair and consistent application of disciplinary outcomes across all departments and work groups. It should be used for all office and fieldwork activities. Because of the subjectivity of the questions, the Tree should be used by a small team or committee instead of a single manager or supervisor. The line between acceptable and unacceptable behavior is clearer when the logic diagram is used. [51]

## Just Culture Decision Tree

```
Was the Behavior → Is the Employee Fit for → Did the Employee → Does it Pass the → Does the Employee have a
Intended?         Duty?                     Knowingly Violate a  Substitution Test   History Unsafe Acts?
                                            Requirement?
(a)               (d)                       (h)                  (l)                 (p)
  ↓                 ↓                         ↓                    ↓                   ↓
Were the           Were Employee needs      Were Requirements    Were there Skill    Was Corrective Training
Consequences       Communicated and          Available, Workable, Deficiencies in     or Counseling Indicated?
Intended?          Clearly Understood?       Intelligible & Correct? Training, Practice,
                                                                  Experience, Feedback,
                                                                  or Selection?
(b)               (e)                       (i)                  (m)                 (q)
  ↓
Was the Action   System    Possible      Possible     System      Possible    System     Blameless
Intentional or   Induced   Intentional   Intentional  Induced     Negligent   Induced    Error
Sabotage?        Error     Violation     Violation    Error       Error       Error
(c)              (f)       (g)           (j)          (k)         (n)         (o)        (r)
```

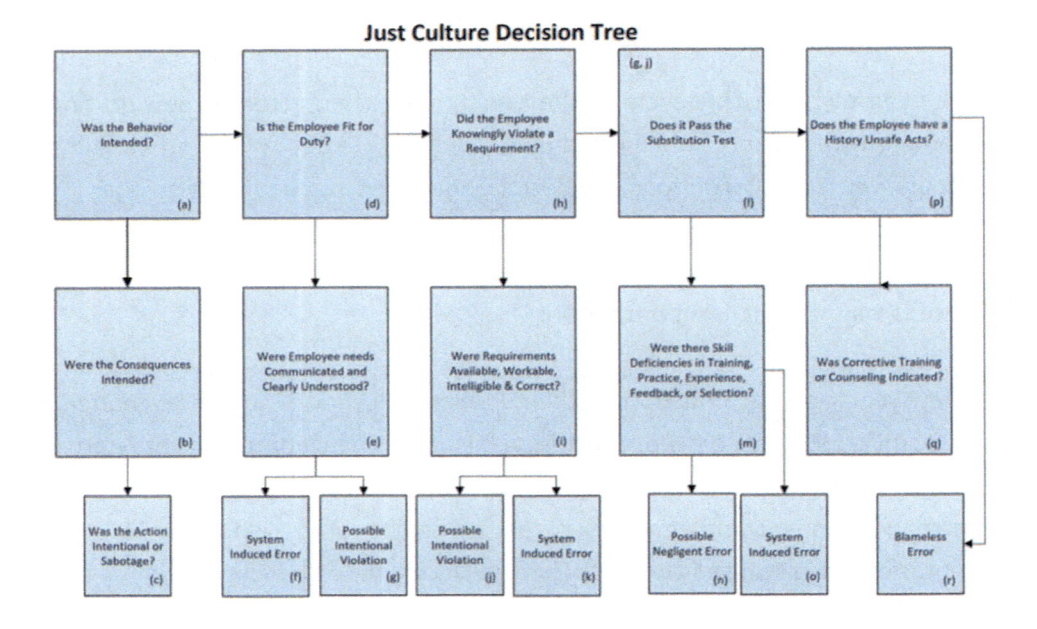

# JUST CULTURE DECISION TREE

Instructions: The diagram is a proven management tool intended to help determine the culpability level of an individual in response to events or near misses triggered by human error. When using the Just Culture Decision Tree, start at the top left box.

a. Be specific on the behavior or action evaluated. For example, if an Operator opened the wrong valve and, as a result, opened several other valves to try to get the event to stop, which behavior or actions would you be evaluating? Evaluate the behavior that initiated the unwanted outcome, looking at intended behavior. In a complex incident, several behaviors that may need to be evaluated individually using the tree. Other than (c), categories should be thought of as blameless, unless they involve aggravating factors not considered here.

b. Typically, the tree is used as the result of a bad outcome. If the answer to "Were the consequences intended?" is no, then progress to (d). If the answer is yes, then exit the tree.

c. Intentional sabotage is grounds for significant discipline or dismissal. An intentional act to cause harm is unacceptable and should receive severe discipline or actions possibly administered by the courts rather than the company. Notify Legal Counsel of these actions. Knowingly violating expectations that were workable likely suggests a reckless violation, a condition that also warrants discipline.

d. Fitness for duty prior to the behavior, including medical restrictions, is to be considered. For example: Was an employee restricted from using ladders or lifting objects over 5 lbs? If the answer is yes, go to (e). If no, go to (h).

e. Were restrictions communicated and clearly understood? In some cases, this can be difficult to determine and may involve interviewing members of the medical staff who noted the restrictions. If it's determined the person did not clearly understand the restrictions, then (e) is no, meaning this was a system-induced error (f). If the answer to (e) is yes, the event is a possible intentional violation (g).

f. A system-induced error is dealt with as such (see also k and o).

g. g) If behavior is determined to be a possible intentional violation, then go to substitution test (l) before determining response.

h. Ensure employee has an opportunity to be interviewed and to provide context to the unwanted outcome before completing this step. Any context provided or statement of fact should be investigated to accurately understand the employee's stated knowledge and intention. If the answer to (h) is yes, go to (i).

i. This is the next level of assurance that the employee was aware that the behavior(s) exhibited did not meet agreed upon expectations. The question should be approached with caution and no determination made until some level of investigation has been conducted into context and circumstances. This may involve interviews with others, review of training records, or an investigation of previous behaviors before the team makes a decision. If the answer to (i) is yes, go to (j). If the answer to (i) is no, go to (k).

j.  If behavior is determined to be a possible intentional violation, then go to substitution test (l) before determining a response.

k.  If the organization did not provide enough detail, information, workability, etc. for the employee to complete the task according to required procedures, then the employee may have unknowingly worked outside the requirements.

l.  The substitution test, or something similar, is used to help in judging the culpability of organizationally-induced violations. This step is the most difficult to understand and apply fairly. The substitution test compares the behavior of the employee being evaluated against an equivalent peer faced with the same context with which the employee was presented to determine whether others exhibit the same behavior (context being the key). This test can be difficult to perform. Use the substitution test as an analysis, not a question, because simply asking peers whether they would have acted in the same way as a peer being evaluated is not considered credible. If (l) is completed via (g) or (j) then stop. If the answer provided by a jury of peers is yes, then the error is likely blameless. If the answer is no, then consider whether there were any system-induced deficiencies in the person's training. If latent conditions are not identified, then consider the possibility of a negligent error. If found, it is likely the unsafe act was a largely blameless system-induced error.

m.  Determine if there were skill deficiencies. The most classic question to evaluate ability is if the employee could not perform this work if their life depended on it. If yes, then a skill deficiency indicates potential system-induced errors such as deficiencies in training, experience, feedback, obstacles, practice or selection. Also consider if the employee has done this before, if so, how often.

n. If the answer to (m) is no, one possibility is a negligent error. Other possibilities may be motivational in nature such as performance is punishing, nonperformance is rewarding, performance doesn't matter, or there are obstacles preventing performance beyond the person's control.

o. For a system-induced error, consider how the system has set the person up for error.

p. Answering no to (p) to a history of unsafe acts could indicate that they made a blameless error (r), something that the employee did not intend to do. If the employee has a history of unsafe acts, it does not necessarily bear on the culpability of the error committed on this particular occasion. It may indicate the need for corrective training or career counseling.

q. Answering yes to a history of repeated unsafe acts may indicate deeper problems, which may also indicate the need for other actions such as changing the job, making the job simpler, on–the–job training, or other options such as transferring or terminating the employee.

r. Something the employee did not intend to do is considered a blameless error. Do not get this confused with no "accountability."

There is always accountability, but discipline or blame is not justified in these cases.[52]

## LEARNING AND IMPROVING IS VITAL. LEARNING IS DELIBERATE.

Before we get into this one, ask yourself one question: "Do I want to know and am I willing to accept the facts I learn?" Many times, people say they want to know certain information, and then when that information is presented to them, they deny what's staring them in the face because it's not what they expected or what they wanted to hear. So, be careful what you ask for. Most companies do what is referred to as a Root Cause Analysis (RCA) any time there is an accident or incident at their company. I know I've done more RCAs than I care to think about. Now, don't get me wrong; an RCA is a great tool, and if used correctly, you will gather some invaluable information. But I can tell you from experience—and any safety professional that has been involved in these analyses will also tell you—many times we go into the RCA with the root cause already determined and we make the exercise fit what we think we already know. These types of investigations can easily be manipulated to fit any story or agenda you want them to. But let's say for a moment that a true Root Cause Analysis is conducted with no prior prejudices or motives involved. Yes, you will determine what the root cause of the accident was. But then what? Well, historically we've NAMED – BLAMED – SHAMED – RETRAINED.

Does this sound familiar?

An accident occurs, so the job, or in some cases the entire jobsite, is shut down. We start our investigation, take photos, get witness statements and interview employees. Once the basic investigation is complete, we do a root cause analysis to determine the cause of the accident. More times than I care to count, I have been involved in determining the root cause of an accident and, in the beginning, what was believed to be "the cause"—or what they wanted it to be—was stated and the rest of the exercise was completed trying to make the events match the cause. Anyone who has ever done a "5-why" or "Fishbone" root cause analysis knows exactly what I'm talking about. These can be very effective tools, but they have to be used correctly. So, we've finished our investigation and determined the root cause of the accident. Our next step is usually to hold an "All hands" safety standdown so we can discuss who, what, where, when, why and how the incident occurred. If the accident was bad enough, then surely some of the top leaders of the company will make an appearance to show solidarity and support.

During this standdown, we tell everyone what the corrective actions will be and usually let the injured employee say a few words just to make sure everyone knows who messed up.

One of the corrective actions will usually be to retrain the employee to ensure they know how to perform the task safely.

I am a firm believer in training. Proper training is absolutely necessary if you want to have a safe company that provides quality work. In some cases, retraining is also required, but not because someone had an accident. I'd be willing to bet that over 90% of this "retraining" is pointless. I mean, did the employee forget how to climb a ladder or how to tie off their fall arrest system? No, of course not. But they'll now spend hours in a class being taught how to do something they already know. What good does this do?

The best way this has ever been explained to me is to think about the game Jenga.

*FIG – 11 Jenga*

Blocks are stacked in alternating directions with three blocks on each level. The first person takes a turn and finds a block below the top level that can be removed and then places it on the top. The players each take turns doing the same thing until one of the blocks is pulled out and the tower collapses. If you think about this as an accident and determine the "Root" cause, its obviously the final block that was removed from the tower, causing it to fall. But is this the reason the tower fell? No, of course not. There were numerous other blocks that had previously been removed and if any one of them had still been in its original place, it's likely the tower would not have collapsed when that final block was taken out.

The last block is considered the root cause and all the other blocks are considered latent weaknesses or even more specific, latent organizational weaknesses. These are the things that lead up to the accident that allowed it to occur. And these are the things you need to identify if you want to create an incident free environment.

Learning first how to approach an investigation is vital, but more so learning where the weaknesses are in your company processes is imperative. Without this knowledge, you will continue to spin your wheels and have the mentality of "what we do is dangerous; accidents are going to happen." That doesn't have to be true.

Everyone learns differently. The four basic ways people learn are seeing, hearing, writing/reading and doing.[53] And sometimes it's a combination of these. No matter your learning style, there are a few things everyone must do in order to truly learn something.

## First, understand you do not already know everything.

This was a tough one for me to learn, especially early on in my career. I thought because I had a college degree, I already knew everything. Boy, was I wrong. I took the Construction Site Safety Technician course and sat through the first week basically daydreaming, because "what could this person possible teach me?" Well, when I got a "D" on my first exam, I realized I wasn't as smart as I thought I was. So, be humble and open your heart and mind so you can learn.

## Next, prepare to learn.

Many people today hear but do not listen. Maybe it's because our world is so hectic and everyone has so much on their mind. Years ago, before the internet and social media, information didn't travel as quickly. But today, something can happen in a remote part of the world and, before the hour is up, the entire world knows about it. So I can understand that people have a lot going on in their heads and it's not easy to just put it all aside. Some people will hear another person's words but are not listening to the *words*; they are listening for the silence at the end so that they can voice a response. Knowledge can't be absorbed if you do this. Put away all distractions (i.e. cellphones, computers, ear pods) and prepare yourself to learn.

## Then, review the information as often as necessary.

Reviewing your notes, relistening to the recording or rewatching the video are a few ways you can review the information. The way I retain information the best is to teach it to others. This method is extremely effective, especially if it's information you want to become an expert in. Years ago, I attended the Georgia Corrections Academy in Forsyth, GA. I was put in charge of a section (approx. 40 cadets) and we would have tests every Monday on the information we covered the previous week. Every Sunday afternoon, I would hold a study session, where I would literally reteach all the subject matter. I graduated as the distinguished honor graduate for my cycle, and it was all because I taught the information to others in order for me to learn it.

## And, lastly, put it into practice.

Take the information you have learned and start using it to benefit you and/or your company.

I have two daughters and they could not be more different from each other when it comes to learning and comprehension. My first graduated from high school and college without studying or, in some cases, without even opening a book. On the other hand, my youngest had to study every night and then cram before the exam just to get through her freshman 101 courses. And for her, learning had to be very deliberate. It didn't come naturally to her, so she had to make a conscious effort to find her learning style and Prepare – Absorb – Capture – Review until she knew the information. Your organization must do the same thing. Make the decision to learn from successes and failures alike.

## HOW YOU RESPOND TO FAILURE MATTERS. HOW LEADERS ACT AND RESPOND COUNTS.

First, let's define failure in this context. Webster's dictionary says a failure is "a lack of success" or "the omission of an expected or required action."[54] But in Human Performance, a failure is not a lack of success. Actually, if responded to in the correct manner, a failure can be a good thing. In Human Performance, a failure is when an error causes a deviation from the expected outcome. Nothing more; nothing less.

Historically, we have been taught to "treat a near miss just like any other incident" and "investigate a good catch the same way you'd investigate an accident." Let's say an employee decides to report a near miss involving a torque wrench slipping, nearly causing him to fall from a platform. He was tied off and all other PPE was being used, so no injuries happened, but the potential injury would have been significant. How do you respond?

- Shut the job down.
- Get witness statements.
- Take photos.
- Interview the employee.

- Perform a Root Cause Analysis.
- Hold an all-hands stand-down to discuss the incident.
- If it was a subcontract employee, you would require the company to provide corrective actions.
- Retrain the employee on the proper way to use a torque wrench.
- Train all employees on the new best practices or procedures resulting from the corrective actions.
- Start enforcing any new rules.

A week later, a different employee has a similar incident involving a "cheater bar" and a 24-inch ratchet. No injury, no property damage and no witnesses. But because of the way you responded to the previous near miss, do you honestly believe this employee will report this one to you? Please don't think I'm suggesting you do not investigate near misses or good catches. What I am saying is that if you "investigate them the same way you'd investigate all other incidents," you will unintentionally discourage the reporting. Put yourself in their shoes. Do you want to be the reason the job is shut down, an all-out incident investigation occurs, there is no way the schedule can be met, and now some "silly new rule" has been added to the already over-regulated process? Of course not! And if employees feel like this, they will not report these things to you.

But, if you gather the information you need without shutting the job down or interrupting the schedule AND then celebrate the fact that it was reported, you will be much more likely to get more and more things reported.

Remember earlier when we talked about a paradigm shift? Well, this is probably the biggest difference you will need to start viewing in a completely different way. Start making the reporting of near misses and good catches a positive thing. The fact is that these incidents—ones that cause no harm or damage to property—are leading indicators and should be treated as such. Another fact: if you have a project site (especially an industrial site) and you have very few or even zero near misses being reported, you're being lied to.

Written by Rod Courtney

I promise they are happening because we are dealing with humans and we all make mistakes. Daily mistakes. And at least some of those mistakes each day are resulting in incidents that are not being reported.

When I was a field safety professional, there was a perception that our leadership didn't truly want to know about every little thing that happened. If there wasn't any blood, a broken bone or major damage to equipment, then we didn't want to know about it. That's not what we said. Actually, we said, "We want you to report every incident, no matter how minor." But come on, we all know that doesn't happen. Because at the end of the week or the end of the job, if too many near misses occurred, then that was a bad thing and must have been an unsafe project.

We have to change this perception and start celebrating Near Miss and good catch reporting. By doing this, the employees see how you respond to the failure and how your company leadership reacts to it. Believe me, this sends a loud and clear message.

I want to reinforce this concept one other way. On February 18, 2001, a famous stock car driver was coming out of turn three at the Daytona Speedway and crashed into the wall, killing him instantly. Who was it? It was Dale Earnhardt, Sr., and even if you've never watched a single NASCAR race, you probably knew the answer to that.

This horrific accident occurred over twenty years ago, and since then, the cars have more horsepower, the potential to drive at speeds 25% faster and wrecks that are so spectacular that some people watch the sport just to see the destruction.

As of the writing of this book, Dale Earnhardt, Sr. was the last driver to be killed in a Sprint Cup race—even over twenty years later, with more power, more speed and definitely wrecks that make evening news highlights almost every weekend a NASCAR race happens.

Let's take our old way of responding to a failure and use it in NASCAR.

- Shut the ~~job~~ race down.
- Get witness statements.
- Take photos.
- Interview the ~~employee~~ race car drivers.
- Perform a Root Cause Analysis.
- Hold an ~~all-hands~~ driver stand-down to discuss the incident.
- Require the ~~company~~ race team to provide corrective actions.
- Retrain the ~~employee~~ drivers on the proper way to ~~use a torque wrench~~ drive a race car.
- Train all ~~employees~~ drivers on the new best practices or procedures resulting from the corrective actions.
- Start enforcing any new rules.

How much sense does that make when you apply it to a stock car race? Every week when an error occurs, we would follow the traditional method of naming, blaming, shaming and retraining. Why not make Jimmie Johnson go through driver retraining if he's involved in a wreck? Because it makes no sense. NASCAR has made the cars, the tires, the tracks, the seatbelts, roll bars and everything else about the sport safer without trying to "fix" the drivers. They've built a system that allows their employees to fail safely. Because it's not a matter of *if* they will fail, it's *when*.

You can do the same thing in your industry.

## CONTEXT INFLUENCES BEHAVIOR AND SYSTEMS DRIVE OUTCOMES.

Context influences behavior?? What does that even mean?? Let me explain it with a short exercise. First, we need to have a few ground rules before doing this.

Written by Rod Courtney

- Go one page at a time.
- Read the directions.
- Come up with your conclusion BEFORE turning the page.
- Don't look ahead at the pages and try to "win." There is no winning or losing. It's just a point I'm trying to make.

*Context influences everything.*

---

### EXAMPLE 1
**Context Influences How We See Shapes**

---

At first glance, which middle circle is larger?

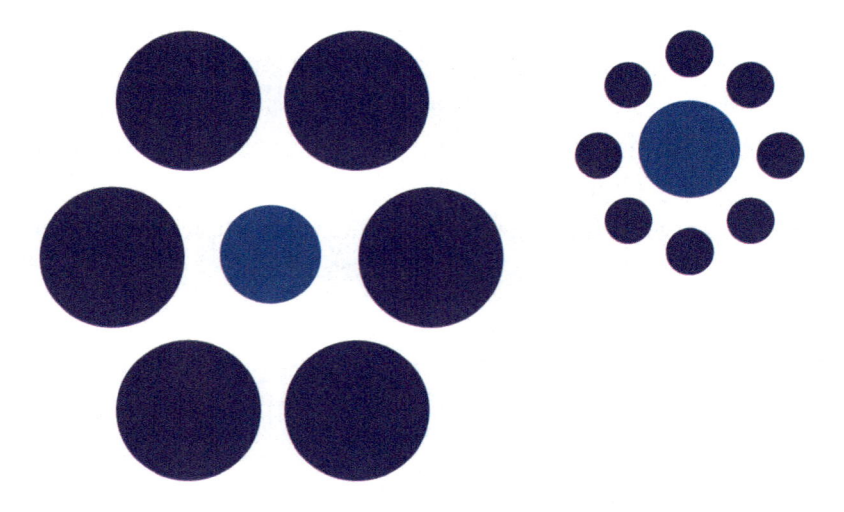

*FIG-12*

At first glance, it appears that the center circle in the diagram on the right is larger. When, in fact, they are the same size.

*Context influences everything.*

---

**EXAMPLE 2**
**Context affects how we see and understand words.**

---

What word do you see?

T A E

*FIG-13*[55]

Obviously, it's the word **THE**.

Now, what word do you see?

C A T

*FIG-14*[56]

Obviously, it's the word **CAT**.

But the "letter" or shape in the middle is exactly the same. But due to the context around it, your brain sees the first one as the letter H and the second one as the letter A.

Written by Rod Courtney

*Context influences everything.*

---

**EXAMPLE 3**
**Context influences how we see emotion.**

---

What emotion is this woman showing?

*FIG-15*[57]

Anger? Yep, definitely anger.

What emotion is this woman showing?

*FIG – 16*[58]

Excitement? Joy?
When all the context is known, then you can understand what the true meaning is.

*Context influences everything.*

---

**EXAMPLE 4**

---

Who's correct?

FIG – 17[59]

Again, context influences how we see everything.

So, context and employee perception are basically the same thing. What do the employees perceive you mean or want when it comes to safety?

*NOTE: In the next few paragraphs, I will direct these ideas and techniques at "you." Just understand that this works for perceptions of people, companies, programs and culture.*

Despite your best intentions, others' perceptions of you become your reputation.

## WHY PERCEPTIONS REALLY MATTER

Resistance to constructive feedback is natural. But regardless of your intent, the impact of your actions on others is real, meaningful, and should be taken seriously. Psychological research into perceptions and behaviors suggests others will treat you and respond in a manner consistent with their perceptions of you. In other words, peoples' perceptions will have real and measurable consequences.

For example, if you are perceived as a bully, others may decide not to include you in teamwork opportunities. If you are deemed untrustworthy, you will likely not be confided in and may struggle to build relationships. Regardless of who you know you are, who others think you are matters.[60]

Always remember: We do not see things as THEY are, we see things as WE are.

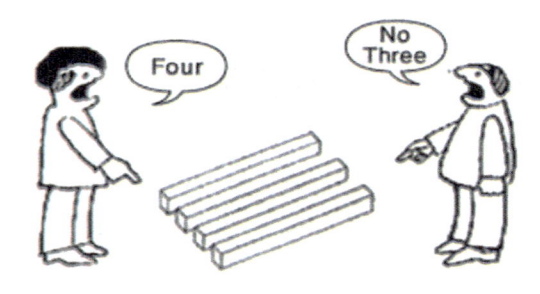

FIG - 18[61]

## HOW TO CHANGE PERCEPTIONS

The first thing you have to understand about changing someone's perception is that you are changing something that they believe 100% to be true. So, if you are in a situation where your intentions and someone's perception of your intentions is different, here are a few tips you can use to fill in the gap.

## 1. Look in the mirror

While your intentions may have been completely different, your communication of these intentions has failed. Don't blame the communicatee, blame the communicator. The best thing you can do in this situation is to ask the person to explain their position. When you ask, always remember to listen to understand not to respond. Then ask these two questions:

- How did my behavior give the impression it did?
- How can I do it differently next time?

## 2. Explain your intentions

Now that you understand how your intentions were misinterpreted, explain things from your point of view. Many times your communication methods had good reasons behind them. Employees are not always privy to everything going on behind the scenes, but when that context is added it can clarify things for everyone.

Our National Sales Manager received a call a few months back from one of our largest clients. In the conversation he could "hear the urgency in his voice" and the client even stated, "I need you to burn rubber on this one." And while urgency was absolutely required, it wasn't until later we realized, it was not to the level we had perceived. We did what we thought the client needed but under the assumption it all had to be completed yesterday. This misunderstanding and lack of context ended up costing our company a substantial opportunity. While this was disappointing, once the client's intentions were better understood, it all made perfect sense.

## 3. Control what you are able to control

There is one thing and one thing only that you are in full control of, and that's how you react to a situation. No one likes to think they are wrong but right vs. wrong is not the goal here. The goal is to become a better version of yourself and if your tone of voice or body posture or even your facial expressions are coming between you and being known as a great leader, then go back to #1 and start over.

Be mindful of your communication style and adjust it as necessary.

## 4. Ask for feedback

If you are trying to change a personal behavior, one of the worst things you can do is ask someone to tell you every time you "act like the old you". All this does is reaffirm to them that you haven't changed and it will, even if only subconsciously, affect how you feel about that person. Negativity breeds negativity.

So, ask them to tell you when you are doing it in the changed manner you agreed to. This is based on Thorndike's Law of Effect. According to this principle, behavior that is followed by pleasant consequences is likely to be repeated, and behavior followed by unpleasant consequences is less likely to be repeated.

By using these techniques, you can surely change perceptions but it's much more effective if you can send the correct message the first time and sometimes this means you have to change your delivery.

44. 44 OSHA, "Recommended Practices," Action item 2.
45. Conklin, 2019
46. AutoCorrectFail.org
47. Merriam-Webster.com Dictionary, "accountability."
48. Merriam-Webster.com Dictionary, "culpability."
49. Varwig, "Human Performance."
50. Conklin 2019.
51. Bush.
52. Ibid.
53. Sphero Team.
54. Merriam-Webster.com Dictionary, "failure."
55. Bush.
56. Ibid.
57. Ibid.
58. Ibid.
59. Taylor.
60. Linnaberry.
61. Picture from https://careeradvancementblog.com/transform-perception/

HABIT #7

# FIND THE STCKY & STOP THE SIF

S.T.C.K.Y. – Stuff That Can Kill You
S.I.F. – Significant Injury or Fatality
P.S.I.F. – Potential Significant Injury or Fatality

In recent years, studies have shown we have done a great job as an industry in reducing the number of injuries in the workplace. If you look back over the past 50 years, you can see the number of recordable accidents has steadily come down, especially since 1992. The average Total Recordable Incident Rate (TRIR) for all industries in 1972 was just under 11 (see graph below). Over the 45 years, that number has steadily dropped and in 2017 was 2.8. While no accidents should be acceptable, that's a pretty darn good trend.

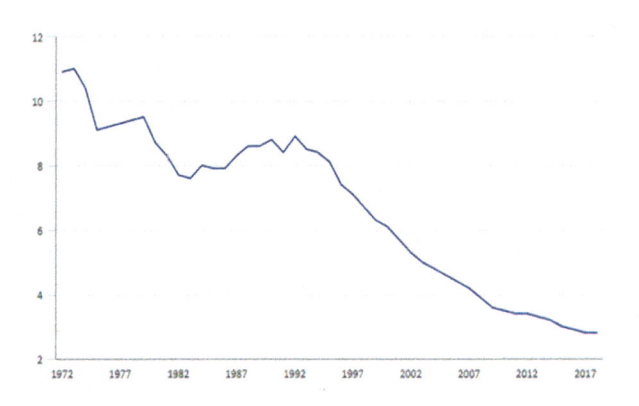

*FIG-19: OSHA Recordable Accidents 1972-2017*[62]

Written by Rod Courtney

In 1992, the U.S. Bureau of Labor Statistics (BLS) started tracking worker fatalities. You would think these numbers would follow the same trend as the TRIR numbers in Figure 19, but you'd be wrong.

**Number of fatal work injuries, 1992–2018**

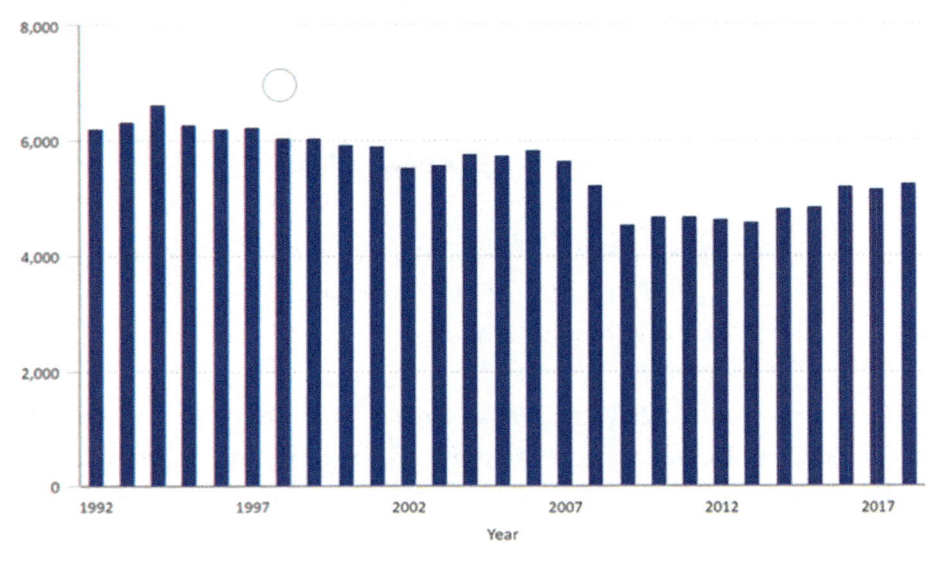

FIG - 20[63]

In 1992, the average TRIR was 8.9 and there were 6,217 work related fatalities in the United States. In 2018 (twenty-six years later), the average TRIR was 2.8, yet there were still 5,250 fatalities. That's over a 300% decrease in cuts, pulled muscles, broken toes and twisted ankles. But only a 16% reduction in fatalities. For the most part, we are killing the same number of people today as we did over twenty years ago. This is not acceptable.

Many scholars have studied the topic of "what kills," and none more so than Dr. Matthew Hallowell. According to Dr. Hallowell's bio page at University of Colorado at Boulder, Dr. Hallowell is a President's Teaching Scholar and Endowed Professor of Construction Engineering at the University of Colorado at Boulder. He earned a BS and MS in Civil Engineering and a PhD with a focus on Construction Engineering and Occupational Safety and Health. Before his academic career, he worked in construction as a laborer, project engineer, and quality inspector.

Dr. Hallowell specializes in construction safety research, with an emphasis on the science of safety. He has published extensively on energy-based hazard recognition, safety leading indicators, safety risk assessment, predictive analytics, and precursor analysis. For his research, he has received the National Science Foundation CAREER Award and the Construction Industry Institute Outstanding Researcher Award.[64]

What he and his team discovered was every fatality is caused by some form of energy. Around 30% of these fatalities happened because the energy that caused them was not identified during the pre-job briefing.

Humans identify and discuss less than half of the energy hazards they will face, not because of lack of effort, but due to systemic blind spots. These blind spots can be addressed via mental shortcuts and simple prompts during pre-job meetings, resulting in improved hazard recognition.

The hazard model many companies have adopted not only aligns with research but also with new safety event classifications that the industry is adopting through Edison Electric Institute (EEI).

## Model Use

- Must be used on the jobsite where hazards are visible and prior to the start of work.
- Must be revisited each day if a multi-day job and reviewed with new workers to the jobsite.
- Must be revised if there is a change to tasks or jobsite that involves a new or altered energy hazard.
- Must be used in conjunction with your current pre-job brief process.

Written by Rod Courtney

### The Hazard Discussion

What is the stuff that can kill you on your jobsite?

What controls are in place to protect you from the stuff that can kill you?

Is that enough protection or do you need more?

## The Energy Wheel

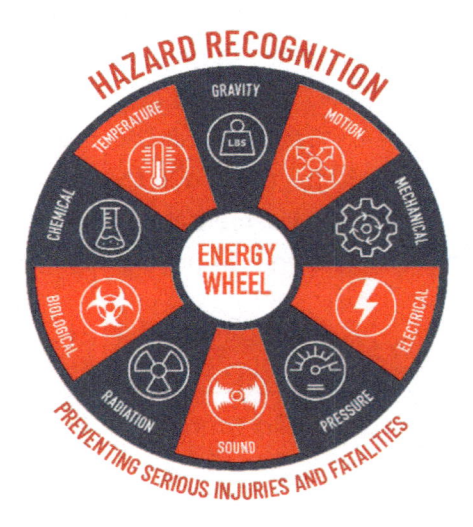

**HAZARD RECOGNITION**

- GRAVITY
- MOTION
- MECHANICAL
- ELECTRICAL
- PRESSURE
- SOUND
- RADIATION
- BIOLOGICAL
- CHEMICAL
- TEMPERATURE

ENERGY WHEEL

*PREVENTING SERIOUS INJURIES AND FATALITIES*

### Mitigation

Ensuring barriers (direct controls) are in place when we make a mistake.

FIG – 21 HAZARD RECOGNITION MODEL[65]

## Best Practices

- Allow brain to recognize the hazards it sees instinctually.
- Use the energy wheel to see what hazards were missed.
- Don't debate about how to classify the hazard.
- Identify the actual hazard, not the energy type.
- Start at 12 o'clock on the wheel and go all the way around.

## Purpose of Coaching and Observations

Coaching is the act of observing and engaging individual behaviors and positively reinforcing desired behaviors and immediately correcting behaviors that do not meet expectations.

## Why Coach?

- Individuals may not know or understand the standards.
- Individuals may know what the expectations are, but are struggling with how to apply them to their daily work.
- Individuals are susceptible to traps.
- Positive reinforcement of expectations will result in consistent performance.

## What a Good Observation Looks Like

- Focus on the facts and the observed behaviors, not the person.
- Behaviors observed should be compared against standards, not personal preferences or perceptions.
- Allowance should not be made because of who the person is or for an overall satisfactory job in which low standards were exhibited.
- Provide timely feedback and ensure it specifically addresses behaviors, not overall performance.
- Reinforce the right behaviors by acknowledging and complimenting workers when positive actions are taken.

Written by Rod Courtney

# Specific for Hazard Model Observations

- Must be used on the jobsite where hazards are visible and prior to the start of work.
- Must be revisited each day if a multi-day job and reviewed with new workers at the jobsite.
- Must be revised if there is a change to tasks or jobsite that involves a new or altered energy hazard.
- Must be used in conjunction with current BU-approved JSA/pre-job brief process.
- Allow the brain to recognize the hazards it sees instinctually, then use the energy wheel to see what hazards where missed.
- Don't debate about how to classify the hazard — identify the actual hazard, not the energy type.
- Ensure that direct controls to mitigate the hazard are discussed (**Not** a direct hazard control — rules, expectations, experience, training, generic PPE, HU tools, warning signs, and cones).

All pre-job assessments start with identifying the steps in the job. Then we identify all hazards involved in each of those steps. And, finally, we identify how we plan to mitigate each of the hazards. What the above hazard model does is ensure all of the STCKY is identified and controlled. It's a simple process of asking, "Have I/we considered this form of energy?" Start at the top of the energy wheel and work your way around it. If any form of energy is identified, just ask, "Do I/we have enough protection from that energy source?" If not, address it. This entire process takes less than 2 minutes on average and reduces the chance you or your employees will incur a significant injury or fatality by 30%.[65]

62. U.S. Bureau of Labor Statistics, Survey of Occupational Injuries and Illnesses.
63. U.S. Bureau of Labor Statistics.
64. CSRA Construction Safety Research Alliance, "Academic Leadership/Dr. Matthew Hallowell."
65. Hallowell 2021.

## HABIT #8
# STOP TRYING TO INFLUENCE EVERYONE

Josh Steimle, the creator of "The 7 Systems of Influence," a framework used by leaders to attract attention, earn respect, and build relationships of trust, said, *"If you try to influence everyone, you won't influence anyone."*

In this chapter, you will learn techniques to influence others, but just remember, if you try to influence everyone, it will be perceived as insincere and you'll end up coming across like a pushy used-car salesperson.

You can have the best written policies/procedures in the world and the best forward-thinking, leading edge principles to guide you. But it all means nothing if they can't be implemented.

Let's be honest; most employees have seen new initiatives come and go. They will not completely buy in until they know it's something that is here to stay. I've heard employees say things like, "It's just another flavor of the month" and, "If we withstand it long enough, they'll forget and we can go back to the way we did it before."

Before we go any further, I want you to know that there is no way to implement these habits correctly, nor is there a way to implement them incorrectly. The only way it will not work is if you do nothing at all.

Written by Rod Courtney

It will take you an average of 66 days to form a habit,[66] so pick one and spend the next one to two months getting it in place. Don't rush it and trust the process.

The first step to being successful is to have visible executive-level support. And that means exactly what it says. The leadership of your company must spearhead the initiative and do so in a very visible way. I've advised clients before by saying, "When the company safety professional walks up to a field crew or group of people, what do the employees expect them to talk about?" The answer is always "safety stuff," and they're correct. I then ask, "When an operational leader approaches the same group of employees, what do they expect them to talk about?" The answer is always "production, schedule or costs." And again, they're correct. What we need is for that operational leader to make a conscious decision to approach employees and talk about safety and whatever initiative you are trying to roll out. See, they expect to hear it from us, but when a "non-safety" leader talks about it, it just carries more weight.

Be sure to train your leaders on the concepts so they can speak about them intelligently and reinforce them with your employees. If possible, start the roll out with something that will be memorable. Get creative, but definitely don't just send an email or memo out to the masses. It needs to feel different and show the company's investment.

Many people are familiar with the OSHA Voluntary Protection Program (VPP) and when they do an initiative roll out, they buy pens, notepads, coffee mugs, stress balls, water bottles, etc. with the OSHA VPP logo on them. I have found that challenge coins and stickers are a great, and inexpensive, way to promote a new idea or program. Have a company cookout or a pizza party, a safety slogan contest or a picnic where employees bring their families. Just something you've never done before to show that **this** is a big deal.

But, no matter how you decide to announce the company's new vision of safety, many will be wondering, "Is this just the flavor of the month?" So be prepared, have a plan that keeps whichever habit you are currently working on at the forefront until it fully takes hold and becomes a part of your organization's DNA. Then, move on to the next one. But, whatever you do, use the habits as building blocks. Don't initiate one, move to the next and forget about the ones you've already created. It is human nature to do what has always been done. How many times have you heard, "That's just how we've always done it?"

Here is my favorite story about how people are conditioned to do things and at some point, we aren't even sure why we do it:

> A group of psychologists performed an experiment involving five monkeys in a large cage. In the middle of the cage, a ladder was placed leading up to some hanging bananas. As the experiment began, one monkey spotted the food and began climbing the ladder. As he did, however, the Scientist sprayed the other four monkeys with ice cold water. As you can imagine, they scrambled around, not understanding why they were being sprayed, screaming and literally bouncing off of the walls. After a while, the banana temptation beckoned and another monkey attempted to climb the ladder. And once again, the researcher sprayed the other four monkeys with ice cold water.
>
> When a third monkey attempted to ascend the ladder, the other monkeys realized that what came next was cold water for all of them. They wanted to avoid this discomfort. Apparently when monkeys are aware that discomfort is imminent, they may not pause to "use their words" ... they cuff, thwack, pummel and drub until the errant monkey gets the message. The monkey climbing the ladder was thus pulled off and educated by the other monkeys.

The second part of the experiment involved removing one monkey and replacing it with a new monkey. As would be expected of the newcomer, upon spotting the bananas, he naïvely began to climb the ladder. And just like the last climber, the other monkeys pulled him off and schooled him.

Here's where it got interesting: The researcher removed a second one of the original monkeys from the cage and replaced him with a new monkey. Again, the new monkey went for the bananas and, again, the other monkeys prevented him from climbing the ladder – including the monkey who had never been sprayed.

By the end of the experiment, all five original monkeys had been replaced with new monkeys, yet, despite none of them ever experiencing the cold, wet, spray, they had all learned never to try to go for the bananas.

And with that, one of the greatest lessons of all time in human behavior was born. The five monkeys' experiment teaches us that we need to be constantly challenging ourselves to look at things from a new light, to question things that don't always feel right, and to avoid using the excuse of "we've always done it this way" to avoid trying new things and branching out in new directions. In other words, if we want that "banana," there are times that we're going to need to get creative, or let those new employees try new things.

Now, this may have been an actual experiment, or it could be an urban legend. Either way, once it becomes a habit, keep it a habit.

Communication is the key to getting buy-in and enthusiastic support from all employees and the ability to effectively communicate is the absolute best skill you can learn. Communicators and influencers, like leaders, are not born. These are learned skills and take time and practice. No matter your line of work or what direction your career is heading, I highly recommend becoming a student of communication techniques. If you first have the ability to communicate, you can accomplish great things.

Why are some people better at influencing than others? Most times, when people approach someone to try and sell them on an idea, they start off by stating their idea and **what** can be accomplished. And, maybe **how** it would benefit the organization. More times than not, they never even discuss **why** it's needed. The problem with this communication method is that it's completely backwards. So while you are explaining what your idea is and how it can be implemented, more times than not, you've lost your audience. See, your audience needs to know "why" first. Then you have their attention and they can visualize your idea just as vividly as you do.

By opening up the conversation with **why**, the listener becomes emotionally involved from the start and will often be inspired, feel a sense of loyalty, and if you then communicate the **how** and the **what** passionately, they will respond accordingly. Here are a few examples to help you practice this communication style.

## WHY - Your Purpose
- Why do we need to have a paradigm shift in safety philosophy?
- Why do we need to do safety differently?
- Why should we buy in to these new ideas?

## HOW - Your Process
- How can we accomplish these things?
- How can we measure progress?

Written by Rod Courtney

## WHAT – Your Result

- What will success look like?
- What will it mean to our bottom line?
- What will it mean for employee morale?
- What will it mean for all our key performance indicators?

**Golden Circle**

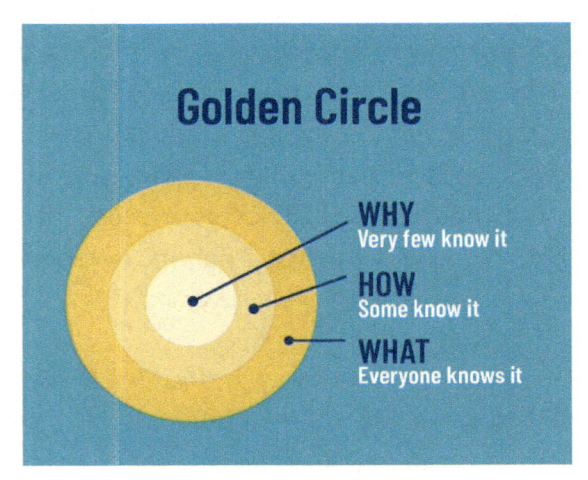

WHY — Very few know it
HOW — Some know it
WHAT — Everyone knows it

FIG – 22[67]

Leadership expert Simon Sinek is perhaps best known for giving one of the most popular TED talks of all time, titled "The Golden Circle." The Golden Circle theory explains how leaders can inspire cooperation, trust and change in a business based on his research about how the most successful organizations think, act and communicate if they start with WHY.

Sinek's Golden Circle model is an attempt to explain why some people and organizations are particularly able to inspire others and differentiate themselves successfully. The neuroscience behind the Golden Circle theory is that humans respond best when messages communicate with those parts of their brain that control emotions, behavior, and decision making.[68]

People like Martin Luther King, Jr., Steve Jobs, and the Wright Brothers had little in common, but they all started with WHY. They realized that people won't truly buy into a product, service, movement, or idea until they understand the WHY behind it.

Most people communicate by stating **what** they want then **how** they want it. Most never even make it to the **why**. But research shows that the most successful people on earth communicate exactly opposite and start with the why.[69]

Now that you have their attention, it's time to explain the **how**. How can this idea be accomplished? What steps need to be taken and how will progress be measured? Out of the three, **why, how** and **what**, how is the least exciting. Be sure to discuss the **how** with enthusiasm because while opening with why makes them "bite," it's how that "sets the hook".

Let's say you want to start an initiative to purchase some software that will allow you to track and trend your safety data.

The conversation would go something like this:

> *Them: Good morning. Come in and have a seat.*
> *You: Thank you, sir. How was your weekend?*
> *Them: It was nice. I had a chance to see my grandson and spend a little time with him.*
> *You: That's great. It's always nice to spend quality time with family.*
> *Them: It sure is. So, what's on your mind?*
> *You: We have been collecting work observation data from sites for a while now, but we're not able to track the information in a way it can be trended.*
> *Them: Yeah, you mean those cards the crews fill out when they observe others working.*
> *You: Yes, sir, those and even the information we get in our incident reports, weekly inspections and monthly project audits. There's a lot of good information just sitting there, but we can't use it because it's*

kept in different places and not kept in a way we can actually track it. If we had the ability to track the information and trend it by incident type or body part or even project site, we would be able to see an accident before it happens and potentially stop it before it ever occurs.

So, you opened up with the WHY. Now the listener can visualize the problem you are trying to solve. Now comes the HOW. Remember it's important to be excited about this part.

> Them: OK, so what can we do about it?
> You: Well, sir, I found a few different systems we can get that will do everything we need, and they are expandable. So, as we grow, they grow with us. The first one is a system called ABC TrackAlot. It has work observations built into it, and when the sites submit them, we can run reports to see exactly what they're seeing in real time. It's pretty inexpensive at $200 per month, and it will work with our current payroll system to keep the employee list updated. I looked at a few others that are really similar to the TrackAlot system, but the one that really stood out to me is one called XYZ Safety Oversight. Sir, this system is the best of the best. It not only lets us do our work observations, but we can also do weekly inspections, monthly audits, incident/accident reports and create corrective action plans for any discrepancy and ensure the issues are addressed. It will work with our payroll system to keep the employee list up to date, and it will also allow us to store all of our safety-related documents in one place. This way, anytime a document is needed it's just a click away for anyone in the office or in the field. Its more expensive at $500 per month, but the cost is minimal considering what we can do with it.
> Them: Sounds like you've done your homework. What kind of contract would we need to sign?
> You: It's an annual agreement up front, and then it's month to month and we can cancel with a 30-day written notice.

Now is time to address WHAT. You got a bite and you set the hook, now let's reel them in.

> *You: Sir, within 60 days, we can have enough data to be able to see an accident before it happens. We can show all stakeholders the results and even show when we meet certain key performance indicators. And lastly, this will help us engage our employees and exponentially increase morale.*
> *Them: Thanks for all the hard work. Get me a contract and I'll review it and we can get this started.*
> *You: Thank you, sir, and thank you for your time.*

I know this hypothetical conversation is relatively simplistic, but the "Why first" approach will work in any conversation where you are trying to influence someone to do something you need done.

Inevitably, you will have some resistance to this new way of thinking and acting. The fact is that no one likes change. You have to commit to being a master of change and not a victim of change. You will surely hear things like:

- I can already identify hazards.
- No added value to this effort, just more paperwork.
- We don't need to change.
- All the other "safety crap" doesn't add value now.

## LEARN HOW TO LEAD YOUR LEADER(S)

What is ~~managing~~ "leading" up?
As I mentioned earlier, you cannot manage people. You lead people. And it's no different in this case either. You're just leading your leader(s).

What does achieving the title of Manager mean? It surely doesn't mean the newly promoted person has the skill sets it takes to be effective. Many times, especially early on in someone's career, they are made a manager because of their expertise in a certain area.

When I was in the Army, I can remember we got a brand new Platoon Leader straight out of college. He was a Second Lieutenant (aka Butter Bar) and while I was an enlisted man and he was a commissioned officer, I had issues with him telling me and my squad what to do and how to do it. We had years of experience, we had all worked together, lived together, trained together and even went into combat together but this young Lieutenant was assigned to lead us. First off, he turned out to be quite the toxic leader, but in the beginning he was just a cocky know-it-all. He thought that because he was an officer and we were enlisted that he somehow was better than us.

Rumor has it that he went into our Company First Sargent's office and complained about him not being saluted when they passed each other. I would have loved to be a fly on the wall and seen how that went over. I can assure you it wasn't pretty, but my point is just because you have a title doesn't make you a leader. There is a step that often gets missed when learning to be or being assigned as a leader, and that's learning to lead your leaders.

So what exactly is leading your leaders, and who are you meant to lead? I've mentioned this concept before and had people react very confused. I mean leaders lead those they are appointed over, right? And traditionally, you'd be correct. "Leading up" means building a positive relationship and making your boss's job easier. Earn their respect and make them look good.

It's not a one way street though. It needs input from both parties and just like any good relationship, a good balance of give and take.

## HOW DOES "LEADING UP" WORK?

The company I currently work for has five owners. One is our President, two are Executive Vice Presidents and two are Vice Presidents. Over the years I have come to know each of their assistants quite well, but the Executive Assistant for our President is quite impressive. She's definitely not the "bring me a cup of coffee" kind of assistant, she's more like a caddy on the Pro Golfers Association (PGA) tour. She takes care of everything except the decision making for the most part. She doesn't have the title but she has more influence in this company than just about anyone else. She definitely has "leading up" down to a science. She's the gatekeeper and she decides who and what gets through to his desk and prioritizes his success over everyone else's.

For most people, "leading up" doesn't involve being so fully ingrained in the details of the leader's life (they probably wouldn't welcome that anyway). However, understanding what matters to your higher-up and orienting toward what helps them succeed should guide your approach to lead your leader.

## THE BENEFITS OF "LEADING UP" IN THE WORKPLACE

Why "lead up?" There are many direct and indirect benefits to learning how to lead your leader(s). Of course you want to have good performance reviews and the ability to be promoted which can lead to new opportunities. But there are also things like your team's performance, completing projects safely, on time, and within budget. These are the things that will help you to build working relationships and reduce stress. By "leading up" you can create a program/system that can basically run itself and the benefits to that are immeasurable. But the reason I wanted to discuss it is because you will need to be able to influence the leadership of your company, because without them spearheading this new way of thinking, it will fail.

Written by Rod Courtney

Mastering the skill of "leading up" it is beneficial to both you and your boss. It means better performance reviews and everything thing comes with that. While this skill set will help you to obtain your personal goals, when done the right way and strategically, the byproduct is you influence employees and leaders alike and ultimately gain the support you need to implement the management system you need for sustainable culture change.

Finally, I will admit that there is a fine line between bragging or being boastful and letting your boss know where you've been successful. In my personal experience, the way I have been able to balance this is to always show my company leadership the accomplishments but never take credit for them. When my name is mentioned with any accolade, I give complete credit to my team. Because without them none of it would have been possible. This does two things: first it shows your leader(s) that you are humble, and secondly it improves moral and the desire to do more within your team.

## BUT THE RELATIONSHIP BETWEEN MY BOSS AND ME IS NOT VERY STRONG.

As I sit here today at my kitchen table writing this book, I can think back to all of the bosses I've had over the years. Probably just like you some of them were terrible in every way, some were average and some were able to bring out the best in me, inspire me and really make a difference in my life.

Long before I learned how to "lead up," I struggled sometimes with bosses that had the need to always talk down to their subordinates and many wanted to take credit for my hard work. The first thing I had to learn is it doesn't matter who takes the credit, it will all come out in the end. This can be very difficult, especially when you are right in the middle of it all. But trust me when I say, it's not about credit, it's about results. Still to this day I have a hard time with the leadership style of belittling and condemnation. These types of leaders are becoming less and less but they do still exist. If your boss is like this the best advice I know to give you is: don't avoid it, face it head on. I know this can be an uncomfortable situation but pretending it's not a problem will not make it go away. So first things first: understand that you are in control of one thing and one thing only in this life, and that how you respond to someone or something. Now, find and admit your own weaknesses and approach the conflict from a "what can I learn from this?" point of view. Then ask your leader for a formal sit down meeting. This meeting does not need to include anyone except you and your boss at this point. But by asking for a formal sit down it shows your boss that this isn't just an insignificant issue that can be resolved at the water cooler.

This meeting can go in a multitude of directions and you will need to be prepared to make decisions as it does. Be open and honest about how your boss makes you feel when he or she puts you down and chastises you. Let them know you are willing and able to do your job how they need you to but you are unclear of the expectations. If this doesn't work you need to be prepared to stand up to them. I am in no way saying to get confrontational with anyone. However, you may need to be prepared to tell them you do not appreciate the way they have talked to you in the past and you would appreciate it if they would do it differently. And lastly, be prepared to stand up and walk out of the room. This takes a lot of guts and may end poorly but there comes a time when toxic leadership will make an employee walk away. It has been said that "employees do not quit their job, they quit their boss." If your boss is that horrible of a leader, you will need to be prepared to do just that.

## "LEADING UP" AND UNDERSTANDING YOUR BOSS

Most of us can feel intimidated by the idea of leading your leader(s) especially if one of them is a, for lack of a better term, a difficult boss as mentioned above. Sometimes you have to become a detective of sorts and learn what makes them tick. What performance indicators are they being held to?

Try to see the world from their perspective, because human nature is to want to know "what's in it for me."

Seeing the world through their eyes can help you influence them and save you a ton of rejection and heartache. Very strategically, ask your boss a few questions:

- What is the most important thing going on from your perspective right now?
- What would make your life easier?
- What keeps them awake at night?
- How would they like to be supported?
- What's their definition of success?

We could probably take this list from five to fifty pretty easily. But the point is to figure out what is important to them, help them solve it and in the process, make them look good.

You don't have to love your boss to get along effectively. Reaching out can be tricky, but try asking a couple of rapport-building questions, such as those mentioned above. It will go a long way to building a relationship with them. When you become the "go-to" person then you can lead your leaders and influence the entire organization.

No matter if you have a toxic leader or a superb leader there are some skills that are universally important. First try to anticipate their needs. This can be tricky but with some experience you will become very good at this. You also need to know what makes the tick and what ticks them off. Problems will come up but knowing how to address it with your boss can help you navigate the situation.

Here is something to always remember: Master the skill of being a genuine source of help. "Leading up" does not mean sucking up. It means being effective and creating value. At the end of the day, that is the way to build the relationships you need in order to influence your organization and its all based on you doing your job and doing it well.

So, we've talked about how to "lead your leader(s)" and now I want to discuss what not to do when trying to influence those above you on the organization chart.

I can't stress this enough: never try to manipulate. All of this must be genuine because being a disingenuous "yes man," always trying to flatter your boss or presenting things as good when they're not are terrible habits and will backfire on you. You can be friendly, supportive, and positive without being manipulative.

Never try to cover something up. Own your mistakes and learn from them. Even when you really don't want to disappoint your boss, eventually the truth will come out.

Years ago I worked for a company finishing up a project. When the job was staffed, it was assigned to the best Project Manager we had and we sent two of our best construction managers plus our Field Operations Manager, who was by far the best construction management person we had on our team. Oh and every single one of them were qualified Safety Professionals on top of their vast knowledge of how to manage a construction site.

On a weekly basis (if not more) the whole team would be asked how things were going and if they needed any help. More times than not the reply would be "No, things are going great; we have everything under control." We weren't getting any complaints from the client so had absolutely no reason to believe otherwise. This went on for many months. We all made senior management visits, spoke with the site team, and the client and everyone was happy.

Well, about six weeks before the project was to be completed, the Project Manager quit and took a job with another company. So our Director of Operations had to step in and take over the PM duties. Then the layers of the onion started to peel off. Not only were their issues at the Project Management level, but the engineering was also a mess and the construction was a complete and utter mess. There were concrete foundations poured that were nine feet off and underground cables that were not in the correct place. They even found an entire scope of work that had been missed and would cost us an additional two-three months.

Had the Project Manager, the Project Engineer, the Construction Managers, or the Field Operations Manager been honest and not tried to hide the fact that the project was heading in the wrong direction, we could have saved millions of dollars and thousands of man-hours on this project.

So when you make a mistake or something goes wrong, don't blame others or make excuses, just own up to it immediately.

Lastly, never ever get involved in office politics or rumors. Leave that drama somewhere else. While at work remember you are always "on stage" and people are watching you. Commit to staying professional at all times. That doesn't mean you can't or shouldn't have a personal conversation your co-workers or even with your boss, but stay firm, fair, and consistent. Never show favoritism and avoid the inner office drama like it is the plague.

Learning how to "lead up" can transform you from just another employee to the go-to person for the tough challenges and growth opportunities. It's a skill that benefits leaders and direct reports at all levels.

Now you know what "leading up" is and why it's important. Plus, you have some actionable tips to put managing up into practice. It's time to give it a try!

Every situation will be different and there is no one way to implement this process. You take the information and just make a difference in your organization even if it's just at a department or single project level.

67. Hallowell 2020.

68. Chaffey.

69. Sinek, 2009.

# THE INCOMPLETE LIST

In Todd Conklin's book, *The 5 Principles of Human Performance*, he talks about a "seven-foot list" that contains the principles of human performance and the safety differently philosophy.

He goes on to say that not everything on the list is actually a principle but more reflective of human performance philosophies and fundamentals.

We know that cultures change and adapt over time. The same is true for human performance and the eight habits we discussed throughout this book. Don't be afraid to change as long as your culture is moving forward and getting better.

Below is the complete "seven-foot list."[70] What would you add to it?

1. People want to do a good job.
2. People are fallible and even the best make mistakes, take risks and drift.
3. Error-likely situations are predictable, manageable, and preventable.
4. People achieve high levels of performance due largely to reinforcement and encouragement from peers, leaders, and subordinates.
5. Individual behaviors are influenced by organizational processes and values.
6. Context drives behaviors.

Written by Rod Courtney

7. People do what makes sense to them at that moment in the context of the work that we help them create.
8. Our organization is precisely tuned to obtain the desired behavior.
9. Events can be prevented.
10. When we choose to learn from events, we can improve.
11. 90% of events are caused by something other than just the individual.
12. People are as safe as they need to be in order to get work done.
13. Blame is the enemy of understanding.
14. Learn or fail again.
15. We can learn and improve or blame and punish, but we cannot do both.
16. Safety is not the absence of an accident but the presence of capacity.
17. Safety comes from making it easy to do the right thing and hard to do the wrong thing.
18. Your reaction matters.
19. Learning is vital to building capacity.
20. Blame fixes nothing.
21. Understanding how and why mistakes occur and applying lessons learned from the past can reduce incidents.
22. The majority of errors associated with incidents stem from latent conditions rather than active errors.
23. Violations of rules and procedures are rarely malicious; but rather, well-meaning behaviors intended to get the job done.
24. Safety has a capacity in organizational excellence.
25. Successful outcomes result from what you do and not implied by an absence of negative outcomes.

*FIG – 24 Lunch on a Skyscraper*

I'm sure most have seen this picture before. It's a photo taken during the construction of Rockefeller Center in 1932. I used to have this picture hanging on the wall of my office, and, boy, what a conversation piece. Some people insist that the picture is staged and it was photoshopped to look like the workers were actually high in the air. Others will say this was just a photo of immigrant workers having lunch while building a skyscraper. My research shows that the photo was staged but is real and not digitally modified or enhanced. But either way, it is an amazing view into the lives of workers during this period of time.

1932 was a very difficult year for everyone living in America. The Great Depression was in full swing and jobs were very hard to come by. If you were lucky enough to have a job, you just put your head down and did what you were told or you'd be fired and replaced within the hour.

Written by Rod Courtney

For just for a minute, let's pretend the year is 1932, and on October 2, we get our copy of the *New York Herald-Tribune* and see this photo. Through the eyes of someone in that generation, what do you see wrong with the picture? If you have your 1932 glasses on, you will see absolutely nothing wrong with it. This was a normal occurrence and men did walk beams 850 feet in the air with no type of protection and sat on the beams to take breaks and have lunch. They had never heard of a personal fall arrest system or safety-toed boots, safety glasses, hardhats or earplugs.

Now let's take off our 1932 glasses and fast-forward time to the present year. We've learned lessons from our past, OSHA has been around for over 50 years and basic human safety actually means something. Now what do you see wrong with the picture? Pretty much everything. Heck, I could write a book based on the violations in this picture alone. We would never work like this today. Workers wouldn't stand for it, and companies would be fined and sued to the point of collapse. We look at this and similar pictures today and say, "What on earth were they thinking?"

My question to you is "What are we seeing today that, ten years from now, we will look back and say, 'Can you believe we used to do it that way?'" At the risk of dating myself, I can remember when safety belts were used for fall protection and iron workers or scaffold builders only had to tie off if they were standing still. So, what are we doing today that future generations will look back and ask, "What on earth were they thinking?"

Now take what you've learned and trust the process.

70. Conklin, "5 Principles."

## AUTHOR BIO

### Rod Courtney

Rod began his career in the U.S. military. He served as an Army Combat Medic from 1990-1998 and attended college at Armstrong Atlantic State University and Columbia Southern University, where he studied Occupational Health & Safety. Rod has been a Certified Safety Technician for 25 years and became a CUSP in 2019. After working for a couple of different companies, Rod went to Iraq with Kellogg Brown & Root in 2003 and was the HS&E Manager for the largest construction project on the planet. In 2007, Rod went to work in the renewable energy sector, building thousands of megawatts of wind turbines and solar plants across the country. He ultimately became the Director of Health, Safety Security & Environmental for one of the largest renewable energy construction companies in the U.S. In 2012, this company merged with another and he decided to start his own safety consulting and staffing firm. Our Safety Guy, LLC was a leader in providing HSE Professionals to wind and solar projects across the U.S. After some soul-searching, Rod and his wife Christi decided to sell the company and find "the perfect fit" with a growing company that had the potential to become a leader in Occupational Health & Safety. He is now the HSE Manager for Ampirical, which is one of the fastest growing companies in the U.S.

Written by Rod Courtney

# REFERENCES

Army Airborne and Ranger Training Brigade (ARTB). "History." U.S. Army Fort Benning website. https://www.benning.army.mil/infantry/ARTB/index.html

AutoCorrectFail staff. Website. https://www.autocorrectfail.org/

Bureau of Labor Statistics. "Injuries, Illnesses, and Fatalities, Table 1." BLS.gov website. https://www.bls.gov/web/osh/summ1_00.htm

Bush, T. Shane. "Human Performance Improvement Handbook." Presentation based on DOE (Department of Energy) Human Performance Handbook.

Cameron, Don. "Evolution of occupational health and safety; when was it introduced?" StaySafe Lone Worker. https://staysafeapp.com/en-us/history-workplace-health-safety-2/

Chaffey, Dave. "Golden Circle model: Simon Sinek's theory of value proposition, start with why." *Smart Insights*. February 3, 2022. https://www.smartinsights.com/digital-marketing-strategy/online-value-proposition/start-with-why-creating-a-value-proposition-with-the-golden-circle-model/

Conklin, Todd. 2012. *Pre-Accident Investigations: An Introduction to Organizational Safety*. New York: CRC Press.

Conklin, Todd. 2019. *The 5 Principles of Human Performance: A contemporary update of the building blocks of Human Performance for the new view of safety*. Santa Fe, NM: Pre-Accident Investigation Media.

CSRA (Construction Safety Research Alliance). "Dr. Matthew Hallowell." Website. https://www.csra.colorado.edu/matt-hallowell

Courtney, Rod. "Safety." *Ampirical.com*. https://ampirical.com/about-ampirical/safety/

Department of Energy. 2009. *Human Performance Improvement Handbook Volume 1: Concepts and Principles*. N.P.

Department of Energy. 2009. *Human Performance Improvement Handbook Volume 2: Human Performance Tools for Individuals, Work Teams, and Management*. N.P.

Frothingham, Scott. 2019. "How Long Does It Take for a New Behavior to Become Automatic?" *Healthline*. October 24, 2019. https://www.healthline.com/health/how-long-does-it-take-to-form-a-habit

Gaynor, Dane. "Motivation Versus Inspiration." Lockheed Martin website. https://www.lockheedmartinjobs.com/space-motivation-versus-inspiration

Hallowell, Matthew. 2020. *Safety Classification and Learning (SCL) Model*. White Paper. March 2020. Prepared for and published by Edison Electric Institute. https://www.safetyfunction.com/scl-model

Hallowell, Matthew R. 2021. "The Energy Wheel: The Art & Science of Energy-Based Hazard Recognition." *Professional Safety*, 66 (12): 27-33.

Ishak, Natasha. "The Story Behind 'Lunch Atop A Skyscraper,' The Photo That Inspired Great Depression-Era America." *ATI* (allthatsinteresting.com). May 18, 2020. https://allthatsinteresting.com/lunch-atop-a-skyscraper

Jarvis, Emily. "5 Leadership Lessons From An Army Ranger." GovLoop.com, October 1, 2014. https://www.govloop.com/5-leadership-lessons-army-ranger/#:~:text=%205%20Leadership%20Lessons%20From%20An%20Army%20Ranger,goes%20wrong%20the%20natural%20tendency%20is...%20More%20

Lally, P., Cornelia H. M. van Jaarsveld, Henry W. W. Potts, and Jane Wardle. 2010. "How are habits formed: Modelling habit formation in the real world." *European Journal of Social Psychology*, 40: 998-1009. https://doi.org/10.1002/ejsp.674

Linnaberry, Eileen. "Others' Perception is Reality – So How Do You Change It?" Vantage Leadership Consulting. Blog. https://www.vantageleadership.com/our-blog/others-perception-reality-change/

MacLaury, Judson. "The Job Safety Law of 1970: Its Passage Was Perilous." U.S. Department of Labor website. https://www.dol.gov/general/aboutdol/history/osha

Merriam-Webster.com Dictionary, s.v. "accountability," accessed April 6, 2022, https://www.merriam-webster.com/dictionary/accountability

Merriam-Webster.com Dictionary, s.v. "advise," accessed April 6, 2022, https://www.merriam-webster.com/dictionary/advise

Merriam-Webster.com Dictionary, s.v. "audit," accessed April 6, 2022, https://www.merriam-webster.com/dictionary/audit

Merriam-Webster.com Dictionary, s.v. "culpability," accessed April 6, 2022, https://www.merriam-webster.com/dictionary/culpability

Merriam-Webster.com Dictionary, s.v. "failure," accessed April 6, 2022, https://www.merriam-webster.com/dictionary/failure.

Merriam-Webster.com Dictionary, s.v. "habit," accessed April 4, 2022, https://www.merriam-webster.com/dictionary/habit.

Merriam-Webster.com Dictionary, s.v. "monitor," accessed April 6, 2022, https://www.merriam-webster.com/dictionary/monitor.

Merriam-Webster.com Dictionary, s.v. "review," accessed April 6, 2022, https://www.merriam-webster.com/dictionary/review.

Morecraft, Charlie. 2009. *Remember Charlie.* Video Recording produced by CharlieMorecraft.com. https://www.charliemorecraft.com/product/remember-charlie-best-seller-safety-video/#:~:text=Released%20in%20early%20October%2F2021,over%20 50%25%20of%20his%20body

Written by Rod Courtney

Nimmo, Ian. "Human Factors and Process Safety." *MyControlRoom.com*, User Centered Design Services, Inc. website. Blog entry.
https://mycontrolroom.com/human-factors-process-safety/

Nixon Library staff. "Executive Orders Issued During the Nixon Administration." *Richard Nixon Presidential Library and Museum*. Website.
https://www.nixonlibrary.gov/president/executive-orders

OSHA (Occupational Safety and Health Administration). "Establishment Search."
https://www.osha.gov/pls/imis/establishment.html

OSHA (Occupational Safety and Health Administration). "OSH Act of 1970."
https://www.osha.gov/laws-regs/oshact/section5-duties

OSHA (Occupational Safety and Health Administration). "Clarification on how the formula is used by OSHA to calculate incidence rates." https://www.osha.gov/laws-regs/standard-interpretations/2016-08-23#:~:text=An%20incidence%20rate%20of%20injuries,Employee%20hours%20worked%20%3D%20Incidence%20rate.

OSHA (Occupational Safety and Health Adminstration). "Recommended Practices for Safety and Health Programs."
https://www.osha.gov/safety-management/hazard-prevention

OUOnline Staff. "8 Ways to Becoming a Better Leader." Ottawa University Business BlogSpot, March 29, 2021. https://www.ottawa.edu/online-and-evening/blog/march-2021/8-ways-to-becoming-a-better-leader#:~:text=%208%20Ways%20to%20Becoming%20a%20Better%20Leader,of%20leaders.%20In%20fact%2C%20a%20recent...%20More%20

Ranger Training Brigade. 2011. *Ranger Handbook*. E-book.
https://www.milsci.ucsb.edu/sites/default/files/sitefiles/resources/Ranger%20Handbook.pdf

SafetyLine Editors. "History of Workplace Safety." *SafetyLine*. Website.
https://safetylineloneworker.com/blog/history-of-workplace-safety?rq=History

Sinek, Simon. 2009. "Start with Why: How Great Leaders Inspire Action." TED Talks 2009. Posted to YouTube August 14, 2012. https://youtu.be/fMOlfsR7SMQ

Sonnenberg, Frank. "Honesty: The Plain and Simple Truth." *Frank Sonnenberg Online.* Website. https://www.franksonnenbergonline.com/blog/honesty-the-plain-and-simple-truth/

Sphero Team. "4 Types of Learning Styles: Explaining the VARK Model." *Sphero.com.* December 8, 2020. https://sphero.com/blogs/news/learning-styles-for-kids#:~:text=The%20four%20core%20learning%20styles%20include%20visual%2C%20auditory%2C,such%20as%20arrows%2C%20charts%2C%20diagrams%2C%20symbols%2C%20and%20more.

Taylor, Jim. "Perception Is Not Reality." *Psychology Today.* August 5, 2019. https://www.psychologytoday.com/us/blog/the-power-prime/201908/perception-is-not-reality

Thomson, Melanie. "Why do we tolerate human over machine error?" *RM Digital Assessment News.* Website. November 20, 2018. https://blog.rmresults.com/why-do-we-tolerate-human-over-machine-error

UENEWS Staff. "Blame the Worker or Fix the Safety Hazard." *UENEWS.* No date. https://www.ueunion.org/stwd_safetyblame.html

U.S. Bureau of Labor Statistics. https://www.bls.gov/

Varwig, David. "Human Performance Overview." PowerPoint presentation highlights EEI Conference April 2009. http://esafetyline.com/eei/conference%20pdf%20files/EEI%20Spring%202009%20PDF/Human%20Performance1_DA%20Varwig.pdf

Wikipedia contributors. "Near miss (safety)." *Wikipedia, The Free Encylopedia.* Last revised March 2, 2022. https://en.wikipedia.org/w/index.php?title=Near_miss_(safety)&oldid=1074859798

Wikipedia contributors. "Murphy's Law." *Wikipedia, The Free Encyclopedia.* Last revised March 20, 2022. https://en.wikipedia.org/w/index.php?title=Murphy%27s_law&oldid=1078290793

Printed in Great Britain
by Amazon